Women at Work

TAVISTOCK WOMEN'S STUDIES

Women at Work

Women at Work

LINDSAY MACKIE
&
POLLY PATTULLO

TAVISTOCK PUBLICATIONS

First published in 1977
by Tavistock Publications
Limited
11 New Fetter Lane,
London EC4P 4EE
Printed in Great Britain
by Richard Clay
(The Chaucer Press), Ltd.,
Bungay, Suffolk

© Lindsay Mackie and
Polly Pattullo 1977

ISBN 0 422 75980 5 (hardbound)
ISBN 0 422 75990 2 (paperback)

Contents

Introduction

What is so special about women's work? Does it differ from the work men do? How far can women be distinguished from men as a separate work force?

The answer is that women's work is radically different from that done by men. Women workers are paid less than men, they work in a much smaller range of occupations, they do much more part-time work, and, in manufacturing, they tend to work alongside other women, in a small number of industries. Women are not as skilled as men, for a variety of reasons, and they are neither promoted as much as men nor are they to be found in great numbers in the professions and in management jobs.

The other huge difference between the bulk of employed men and most employed women is that women are generally considered responsible for the maintenance of home life and the care of children. In spite of the dramatic rise in the numbers of women – particularly married women – going outside the home to work (40 per cent of all married women are now employed compared to 10 per cent in 1931) the full implications of what is an appalling double burden for millions of women have not been grasped by our society.

The *Equal Pay Act* and the *Sex Discrimination Act*, along with other legislation designed to improve the lot of women, will not themselves bring true equality in work between men and women. This will only come if women are able to escape from the low paid, unskilled jobs in which they are mainly concentrated and if this escape is reinforced by a radical change in relationships between, and roles of, men and women both at home and at work.

We would like to thank the many men and women in trade unions, factories, companies, universities, and research organizations who gave us their time, information, and advice. In particular we are grateful to the members of the Department of Employment Library and the Fawcett Library. We are also indebted to Sue Mallett and Garry Todd who helped us type the manuscript. To members of the women's movement we also owe a great deal.

ONE

Housework : prison or holy vocation ?

The history of housework is poorly documented for the voices of most women down the centuries are silent. We know very little about how women felt about their work in the home, with the exception of a few upper-class women who had the opportunity to write diaries or who were important enough to be written about by others. But we do know what women did, or at least what they were expected to do. There is no shortage of homilies, written by men, about the 'gentle' sex and their duties. The Becon Boke of Matrimony, 1543, for example, states that the wife's duties to her husband are 'to serve him in subjection, to be modest in speech and apparel, to have charge of the house and its management'.

If women were then subjected – as they often are still – to the caprice and demands of their husbands, there was one crucial difference. Before the industrial revolution women were one half of an economic unit, that of husband and wife. The division of labour in the home as it was created and perpetuated by capitalism, was then unknown. Home and work were inextricably linked. Often men and women worked at home, so the home was the productive unit. 'The home and the outside world were one; real life was *domestic*. It was concerned with survival in a hostile environment and depended on the skill and effort of every member of the community, regardless of sex or age' (Comer 1974:74).

To describe housework up until the middle of the seventeenth century is to describe the whole spectrum of woman's life: it was neither compartmentalized, isolated, or solitary. 'Their labour was visible and was seen by all as necessary (though perhaps inferior) complement to the labour of the father and husband' (Gardiner 1975). Woman's work in a rural family was gruelling and virtually unending, but it was also creative, productive, and responsible. This is an extract from the Boke of Husbandrie by Sir Anthony Fitzherbert, 1555:

> 'First ... get all things in good order within thy house, milk the kine, suckle thy calves, strain up thy milk ... get corn and malt ready for the mill to bake and to brew ... Thou must make butter and cheese when thou may, serve thy swine both morning and evening ... March is time to sow flax and hemp ... it should be sown, weeded, pulled, watered, dried, beaten, braked, hatcheled, spun, wound, wrapped and woven.'

Fitzherbert continues to describe how a wife should always have her distaff ready to spin either wool from the husband's sheep or to take wool from cloth makers. (The word spinster originally denoted a woman whose trade was spinning.) Then there was harvest time when the wife had 'to make hay, to shear corn'. Going to market to sell domestic products, to buy goods for the house and to account expenses and payments to her husband were also wifely duties.

Virtually all agricultural work was open to women of the farmer and husbandman class – for example, sheep shearing, thatching, brewing (this last was a task exclusive to women). These women carried considerable economic status, and when land in the early American colonies was being carved up, double the amount of land was given to a married couple than to a single man.

There were, of course, the wage-earners, the families of the landless farm labourers, whose lives were blighted by poverty. And it was the women and her children, in particular, who suffered. The labourer was usually given sufficient food and drink to keep him fit enough to do his job, but his family went without. The sufferings of the woman were acute, often she was half-starved, and of the many children born to her, few reached adulthood.

The children of the labouring poor, and single women, often became servants in richer homes, hired by the woman of the house. She was the queen of an extensive empire. She hired and fired the servants, trained and cajoled them, kept the accounts, and generally supervised the workings of the estate. In 1689, a French woman, the Comtesse de Rochefort, whose husband – as was common – was away in the army, kept a diary of her day-to-day life. Here are some of the details from her diary. She wrote to the attorney about a pending legal case. She examined the woods to estimate the value of the part that was for sale. On June 1 she received payment from the butcher for mutton and beef, inspected the crops and discussed sowing times with a tenant, started urgent work on two millstones, and 'got the carders in to work on a hundredweight of washed wool'.

The women of the British aristocracy led similarly responsible lives. They had not yet retreated to the drawing-room. The Civil War memoirs of the Verney family quotes Lady Barrymore:

'A cuntry lady living in Ireland and convercing with none but masons and carpendors, for I am finishing a house, so that if my gouvenour please to build a new house, that may be well seated and have a good prospect, I will give him my best advice gratis.'

(Clark 1919:14)

The strength of the woman's position was that psychologically the man too identified with the home – it was also his economic base. And the design of the home contributed to the integration of the family. Houses were not divided into rooms. The hall, which was the entrance to the house, was the centre of domestic life. Kitchens and bedrooms were not separated off. In upper and middle-class homes there were some thirty to forty people sleeping, eating, and living together. Children were not the sole responsibility of their mother. Men took an interest in the rearing and education of children and many had had first-hand experience of childcare and domestic work because often young men were sent off to work in other families. These sort of living arrangements did much to release women, at least the comfortably off ones, from a great deal of household drudgery.

Yet authority, in the family, rested squarely with the husband. Patriarchy had an unblemished heritage, and the evidence of the Bible and religious practice could bring a wayward wife to heel. William Gouge in 'Of domesticall duties', wrote in 1634: 'Though an husband in regard of evil qualities may carry the image of the devil, yet in regard of his place and office, he beareth the image of God.' Ironically, though, it was through religion that the first cracks appeared in this particular model of law and order. Excluded from a role in either the Church of England or the Catholic Church, women turned to the new religious sects – Quakers, ranters, Baptists – who preached spiritual equality between the sexes and allowed, even encouraged, women to preach and participate in religious life. Through their sectarian activities they inched towards secular equality. 'We will not be wives, and tie up our lives, to villianouse slavery', ran the chorus of a skit in 1662. It was only a small skirmish, and it was not yet enough to make a successful challenge to domestic order.

But then married women had no rights to property, and on marriage their goods and chattels passed to their husbands. However, husbands needed wives, not just to bear children, but for an economic role. 'The wife was subject to her husband, her life was generally an arduous one, but she was by no means regarded as his servant' (Clark 1919:41). Women's lot was not then one of economic servitude; the quotation shows that however untenable many aspects of a woman's life then was, her domestic role was not secondary or passive.

So, then, there was a time – if not a pastoral idyll – at least a period of strength for women when they were not seen as primarily sexual objects on the one hand nor domestic drudges on the other. The women of the suburban coffee mornings of today would have felt out of place among the business-like farmers' wives of the seventeenth-century market place.

But the vitality of women was soon to be destroyed, and did not survive the new eighteenth century. What did happen to swamp women's domestic, economic role was the industrial revolution that for nearly two centuries polarized women: upper-class women removed themselves from practical household management to the drawing-room, while the industrial revolution claimed working-class women for its own.

The idea that a woman's place is in the home took firm root in Victorian Britain, and that belief is still with us. The capacity of many Victorians for self deception was unbounded, and no clearer evidence of this hypocrisy exists than in the discrepancy between the idealized picture of Woman, and the fate of those millions of women who had to go to work outside their homes. In 1851, the year of the first proper census there were eight million women over the age of ten in Scotland, England, and Wales. These were the women and female children of working age, and 2,348,200 of them went out to work – that is, a quarter of the female population was doing work quite unrelated to that popularly considered fit for them to do. But then the myth was created by and for the powerful middle classes, and their wives did not go out to work, although their unmarried daughters might have to suffer in genteel despair as governesses.

So, during the period that the belief in the little woman being incompetent or unsuitable for outside employment was at its height, a quarter of these incompetents were in employment, admittedly appallingly paid for the most part, and only semi-skilled in the majority.

What did Victorian working women do? Overwhelmingly they worked in other people's homes, and one of the odd, cruel ironies of the doctrine that women were destined for the home was that it kept hundreds of thousands of women enslaved in miserable conditions in homes which were not theirs, and which required a staggering amount of physical labour to keep them in the necessary sparkling condition. At the same time as 13 per cent of the working population (in 1851) was engaged in housework, the Victorian middle-class woman had less and less to do with the actual running and detailed control of her own home. In *Not in Front of the Servants*, Frank Dawes says,

'A dishonest cook or housekeeper had ample scope for

cheating because she gave orders to tradesmen and kept the books. She controlled the stores, the still room and the linen cupboard. Most ladies only inspected the books once a week and any self-respecting cook expected advance notice if the mistress intended to descend to the kitchen.'

(Dawes 1973:59)

Domestic service was 'women's work', although it was a sign of great affluence to have male servants, and in 1881 there were 1,269,000 women in 'service' with another quarter of a million doing charring and washing.

In the last quarter of the century it was estimated that one in every three girls aged fifteen to twenty was a domestic servant (Best 1973:124) and in 1881 10 per cent of the entire female population of Britain was employed 'below stairs' in someone else's home.

The woman servant was not a status symbol in the way that a male footman, for instance, was. Women were kept indoors and out of sight, tweenies and cooks and housemaids not being ornamental nor symbolic of wealth. They were paid less than male servants and were often curtailed in their private lives – being forbidden boyfriends, or 'followers', as the phrase went. Mrs Beeton in 1861 thought that the wages for a housekeeper should be £18–£40 a year, for a cook £12–£26, for a housemaid £10–£17, and for the poor little maid of all work £7.10s–£11. Flora Thompson, in her autobiographical work *Lark Rise to Sandleford*, writing about her childhood in a Oxfordshire village, gives a touching picture of the start of a working life for many country girls.

'There was no girl of 12 or 13 living permanently in the village. Some were sent to their first place at eleven. The way they were pushed out into the world at that tender age might have seemed heartless to a casual observer. As soon as a little girl approached school leaving age her mother would say "About time you was earning your own living me gal". From that time onward the child was made to feel herself one too many in the overcrowded home, while her brothers, when they left school and began to bring home a few shillings a week, were treated with a new consideration and made much of.'

(Thompson 1973:155)

Their money meant a little more for the family purse and every shilling was precious. The girls, while at home, could earn nothing. The largest proportion of domestic servants in the nineteenth century came from among the daughters of the agricultural poor. There was another kind of woman employed in the home too, but she was the baby minder, often simply a little girl of nine or ten, paid a few pence to look after the children of women working in the factories.

There were thus two kinds of Victorian homes. One in which daughters were thrust out to work as soon as was humanly possible, where many married women went out to work, and where a man's wage alone would have meant starvation. The other kind was the home of the antimacassar, the calling card, the servants' quarters, the five-course dinner, and the elaborate entertaining.

What were they *for*, these superb middle-class homes? They really were simply not practical. People could have lived in comfort with less of almost everything. It is, after all, a wasteful society which takes as its household manual a book 2,000 pages long. Were the homes of the middle classes, then, their symbols, their barricades against insecurity, their marks of confidence?

What they undoubtedly were primarily were cages for Victorian wives, whose aim in life was thought to be 'securing the permanent happiness of the little kingdom in which she reigns and lighting up with the brightness of content and satisfaction the face she most loves to see'. The comforts of an upper-class home drove Florence Nightingale in 1846, at the age of twenty-six, to write:

'I am up to my chin in linen, glass and china and I am very fond of housekeeping. In this too highly educated, too little active age, it is at least a practical application of our theories to something – and yet in the middle of my lists, my green lists, brown lists, red lists, of all my instruments of the ornamental in culinary accomplishments, which I cannot even divine the use of, I cannot help asking in my head "Can reasonable people want all this?" '

(Woodham-Smith 1953:50)

She also wrote that she knew women who had gone mad for lack of things to do, and in a further savage criticism, and one

15

which is stunning in its modern tone she wrote:

> 'Women don't consider themselves as human beings at all.
> There is absolutely no God, no country, no duty to them at
> all, except family ... I know a good deal of convents and of
> course everyone has talked of the petty grinding tyrannies
> supposed to be exercised there. But I know nothing like the
> petty grinding tyranny of a good English family. And the only
> alleviation is that the tyrannised submits with a heart full of
> affection.'   (Woodham-Smith 1952:71)

The home for the middle-class Victorian family, at least for
its male head, seems in retrospect also to have been a kind of
toy, with the little woman in a kind of mock command. Read
any of the popular household encyclopaedias of the nineteenth
century and the overpowering impression is that of the fascina-
tion with objects, with techniques, with transforming materials,
with adding to the great stock of physical objects everywhere.
It was partly a reflection of the inventiveness of the time, of
human control of environments and it was acted out within the
home. A marvellous book, published in 1850, *The Household
Book of Domestic Economy*, shows all this. It overflows with
suggestions on making cheap violins, engraving figures on glass,
tinning objects, preserving lemons, making traps for snails, con-
cocting a 'pleasant cordial for low spirits' (in which one of the
items is two *gallons* of spirit), making milk of roses, reviving
withered flowers, removing stains from mourning dresses, applying gold leaf to leather, and so on and on.

A book written by one Henry Southgate, coyly entitled
Things a Lady Would Like to Know, is also filled with information. Mr Southgate confesses his leaning towards simplicity. His
suggestion for a simple August dinner for guests is as follows:
mock turtle soup, fillets of sole with white sauce, eels with
tartar sauce, sweetbreads, mushrooms and potato balls, sirloin
of beef, french beans and potatoes, Zandrina pudding, rice
fritters, savoury macaroni, cheese, salad, etc.

The pressure that was built up to push women into their myth-
ological mould was considerable. Mrs Beeton may have devoted
2,000 pages to the management of the home, but she still re-
ferred to the 'little worries' of domestic life, which were, of
course, dwarfed by the concerns of the man outside the home.
She wrote:

'We cannot too strongly insist on the vital importance of always preserving an equable good temper amidst all the little cares and worries of domestic life. Many women may be heard to declare that men cannot realise the petty anxieties of a household. But a woman must cultivate that tact and forbearance without which no man can hope to succeed in his career.'

In *Things a Lady Would Like to Know*, the author puts mottoes at the introduction of each day's menus. For March 29, he chose this maxim:

'Eccentricity in women is totally out of character. Neither genius, wit, generosity nor even honesty can make up for it. So peculiarly does the real power of a woman depend upon her power of pleasing and so exclusively does that depend upon softness.'

There were, among the women to whom such advice was directed, exceptions. There were many in the upper classes – like Caroline Norton, who was instrumental in changing the law in order to allow mothers custody of their own children; like Florence Nightingale, and like Victoria Sackville, mother of Vita Sackville West, who took over the management of her father's estate, went into business, made money, and won lawsuits.

It was harder for the middle-class woman. Anthony Trollope's mother supported herself and her family when it became clear that her husband was utterly incompetent to do so, but still she kept up the pretence that it was she who was the clinging vine in their marriage. For the 28 per cent of women in the Victorian era who did not marry, life could be very grim. They could become governesses, or they stayed in thrall in their parents' home, doing meek little tasks, at everyone's bidding, without rights or status of their own. As the century advanced, more women went into teaching. By 1881 there were 6,000 female clerks, and a meagre 38,000 nurses.

However, the woman at home had become a mark of success for her husband, so that by 1911 only one in ten married women worked, where one in four had worked outside the home in 1851. Legislation protecting women working in factories had cut their hours, and decreasing poverty had meant more families could exist on the man's wages alone. In terms of sheer physical work this was an improvement, but was it double edged? Sheila Rowbotham thinks it was a barbed blessing.

'The need for women's labour in the family thus exercised a certain restraint on the direct exploitation of women's labour power in industry. But women's social usefulness was never recognized or recompensed. Instead their dependence on the male bread winner and their work in the family reduced their capacity to organize. They were thus placed at a double disadvantage.'   (Rowbotham 1973:58)

One of the greatest changes of twentieth century life in Britain has been the great decline in the proportion of women who work only in the home. Today 62 per cent of employed women are married. The largest increase in the numbers of married women working has occurred in the years since the Second World War, and since 1961 alone a further 10 per cent of all married women have decided to go out of the home to work.

One reason for the rising proportion of married women going out to work – it is now over 40 per cent – has simply been that marriage has become more popular. Compared to 1931, when 59 per cent of the women aged twenty-five to twenty-nine in England and Wales were married, the figure for 1966 was 87 per cent in the same age group.

The demand for labour in the manufacturing service industries has greatly increased, and the other side of the economic coin has been that people have felt the necessity of two incomes to support a home. For the mother supporting a family on her own – and this figure too is rising – the necessity of employment is obvious. Another reason, which is almost impossible to present with any degree of objective confidence is the isolation, the loneliness, and the drudgery of housework. The argument is a risky one, because it ignores economic urgency, but it crops up so often in conversations with women who work only in their homes that it must be a substantial factor in the rising employment figures for married women, particularly for those with children. Ann Oakley (1974) in *The Sociology of Housework* quotes a table which indicates that more housewives in a sample found housework monotonous than assembly line workers found their jobs dreary. This is a savage indictment of the work too often thought to be 'natural' for women to do.

This isolation is perhaps most acute for the estimated 300,000 single women who care for elderly parents or relatives. They have often given up employment to do so – and thus may end up with neither income nor pension rights. Furthermore they do not have the status marriage confers, nor the companionship it can bring; yet their work in the home is arduous and constant.

Housework – taken to include everything which is done to organize and care for a family and a home – is today a depressing task compared to what it was even fifty years ago. The difference seems to lie in the value attached to housework by society and so to the person doing the housework. 'I'm only a housewife' is a famous, modern remark. And although millions of women do their jobs as housewives with pride and efficiency, it does seem often to be in spite, rather than because, of the nature of the job. It is telling to compare an excerpt from a modern book of household management with the tone – however patronizing or pretentious – of Victorian books of the same class. 'It's amazing how much better a room looks if you *don't clean it at all*, but simply tidy it, straightening the cushions, emptying the ashtrays and shoving every odd thing into a large basket and standing it in a corner' (Conran, 1975:20). The Victorians treated housework as a glorious task. Ms Conran shows it, no doubt quite properly, as something which ideally should be an avenue of short cuts.

But there is no time limit on housework. The housewife seems nothing more than a perpetual motion machine. The work she does is a continuous process which can never be left for a day off. In Ann Oakley's survey of forty housewives she found that their average working week was seventy-seven hours, the maximum hours being 105 and the fewest forty-eight. The latter was done by a woman who had a full time job outside the home (Oakley 1974:183).

Work also expands to fill the time available. 'The modern American housewife spends far more time washing, drying, and ironing than her mother. If she has an electric freezer or mixer, she spends more time cooking than a woman who does not have these labour saving devices. The home freezer, simply by existing, takes up time ... elaborate recipes with pureed chestnuts, watercress and almonds take longer than broiling lamb chops' (Friedan 1965).

A housewife is responsible for running a home. She cooks, cleans, shops, cares for clothes, organizes expenditure, keeps an eye on the fabric of a house. She is usually responsible for the care of children and is expected to support her husband. From her is derived the image of the home that is presented to outsiders. The woman is more likely than her husband to dictate the choice of furniture, decoration, and the degree of comfort of the home. So the home and the work it involves is an expression of the woman's identity, but it often ends up by being the sole expression of that identity.

Being a housewife means being economically dependent on someone else and in a society where money is the way in which work is rewarded, and its importance recognized, being an unpaid worker has undermined woman's status in the eyes of society. It has also harmed the image the housewife has of herself and brings tensions to her job. 'Before I went out to work, all our rows were about money. We'd row if I asked for a few shillings for a packet of cigarettes' (Maureen Baines, housewife).

Women may control the household budget but they rarely feel free to take money out of that sum, as of right, on a regular basis, to spend on their own individual needs. In very few families is an allowance set aside solely for the woman. Furthermore, large numbers of women are not even aware of how much their husbands earn. The acute financial dependence of housewives and the assumption that they have no right to know how much money is available for home and family was illustrated in a survey which found that, despite a national wage increase and inflation, the household allowances in a substantial proportion of cases had not been increased at all (National Opinion Polls, September 1975).

Even if housework were a paid activity – and this would only reinforce the idea that housework is woman's work – the nature of a housewife's work would not really change. The hours would continue to be long, and the tasks would remain the same. Women in the home would still be cut off from each other and from the world of employed men and women.

Many women have become more isolated than ever before in the home. The main reason for married women not taking up outside employment is that they are responsible for children. The General Household Survey of 1971 found that over 90 per cent of those women who intended to get a job in the future were not currently working outside the home because they had to care for their children. But a third of these women 'would have brought forward their plans to return to work if satisfactory arrangements could have been made to look after the children' (Department of Employment 1974:14).

The care of children is not in itself an isolating nor demeaning activity. But for many women it has become more of a burden. Women can no longer rely, as many of them once did, on cooperating with aunts, mothers, sisters, and cousins in bringing up children.

'All my family lived around Denby Street,' said Mrs Harper, 'and we were always in and out of each other's houses.' Every day Mrs Harper dropped in on one sister or another and saw a niece or an aunt at the market or the corner shop. People always dropped in on her, and at her confinements, 'all my sisters and the neighbours used to help'. However, when Mrs Harper moved to a new estate in Essex, life changed radically. 'I tried getting friendly with the woman next door but one, but it didn't work.' It is the loneliness she disliked most – and the quietness that she thinks will in time 'send people off their heads' (Young and Willmott 1957:107).

Hannah Gavron in *The Captive Wife* (1966) found that both middle-class and working-class women shared feelings of being tied to the house and cut off from social contacts. Women's magazines, too, recognize the problem. *Woman's Own* spelt it out in an article on mental breakdown: 'If you are homebound and therefore lonely, feeling useless and unworthy, then make a conscious effort to escape the trap of your own four walls.'

'If you're getting on well with your husband then the job becomes more interesting. If it's going badly, the depressions multiply. It's vital to have lots of outside friends, but it's difficult because there just aren't any single men and in lots of couples we know I can't stand one of them. If you are fed up and go and see a friend – nine times out of ten she has children and you've got your child and you can't hold a conversation line for five minutes. It does have its grossly humorous side, I suppose.'   (Sally Corfield, housewife)

Women have different ways of coping with this isolation. Theresa, twenty-six, mother of two small children: 'You'd get like a cabbage if you only did housework. I do a lot of writing in my diary. I don't know what other people do.'

Marion, thirty-five, with two small children, and two cleaning jobs to go to, said she went to school to collect her children half an hour earlier than she needed to, 'to chat to the other mums'. Those other mothers felt the same need. Marion's diary for any weekday is as follows:

'I get up at 3.10, come downstairs and have a cup of tea and a fag. I start cleaning at 4.15 and get home after 8. I call my husband and the children, dress the kids and run around. I make the breakfast and have it with them. I take them to school and at 9.30 I'm at my second job. I finish that at 10.15, come home, have a cup of tea and a look at the paper. I make the beds, wash up the breakfast things, do a bit of shopping for a loaf of bread and things like that, and clean up. Then I have a look at the kids in the playground to make sure they're alright. At 12.30 my husband comes back from work and I make a sandwich for him. Then I wash up the cups and plates and do a bit of washing by hand – the big wash I do in the machine – and then I prepare the kiddies' dinner and pick them up from school at 3.30. While I'm waiting for them I like to talk to the other mums. At 4.15 I finish cooking dinner. My husband, he's a roofer, he comes in at about 5.00. We all sit down and have dinner and a cup of tea. Then I wash up and my husband dries or he washes up too. At 6.00 everyone is quiet for the news on TV. Then I listen to the children read or we have a spelling competition. At 6.30 I watch Crossroads and no one but no one disturbs me. We've got another TV in the front room so that I can watch it alone. At 7.00 the kids and I have a bath. At 7.30 the kids go to bed. We have a cup of tea. Then I sort out the school uniforms and make sure the clean clothes are ready. 8.30–8.45 I read the paper. By 9.00 I'm ready for bed. 10.00 is the absolute latest for me.'

When housework is combined with the care of young children a woman's time and thoughts are not her own, although the tasks she is doing may not be particularly complicated or physically arduous. It is a tiring process.

'I work from 8 in the morning till 10 at night, seven days a week. Some of it is enjoyable and can't be called hard work, like gardening or playing with Phillipa. What is really arduous is intensive cleaning and having children always in the background. I don't know if any other housewife has said this to you, but it's hard to switch off. There's a sort of gentle tension all the time. You always have an ear or an eye on what's going on. And there's the interminable "What are you doing? Can I have a sweet?" – I don't know why it is so tiring, but it is.'

(Sally Corfield)

The idea of men and women sharing both daily parental and household responsibilities is gradually acquiring a more conventional aspect. In 1975 the Greater London Council decided to allow paternal leave on the birth of a baby, for a few days only, but it was a recognition of both a father's needs and, perhaps, his role as a working member of a home.

In the 1960s Hannah Gavron found that the husbands of the women she interviewed were spending more time sharing household tasks than they had before – 54 per cent of working-class husbands did some household work, and 21 per cent of the middle-class husbands in her sample. Yet in 1975 Shirley Conran could still write in *Superwoman*: 'A man who doesn't mind the occasional snack in a crisis – or even cook it – is worth his weight in platinum, giving a clear indication to her readers how she felt responsibility in the home should be divided. And gratitude to their men for helping in the house is often expressed by women. 'I'll give him his due, there aren't many men who'd bath the children. Mick can do the dinner and wash and iron his clothes. But, poor sod, he works all day so why shouldn't I cook him a meal and iron his shirts?' (Theresa, housewife).

Ann Oakley found that the housewives she interviewed felt that the autonomy of their job was the most valuable and positive aspect of it. In day-to-day work they were not accountable to anyone but themselves, they could choose when to do the cleaning and when to do the washing. Nineteen of her respondents said that 'being your own boss' was the best thing about the job. They also valued looking after children and having free time (Oakley 1974:43).

But this autonomy is circumscribed. There are the demands

of children and the needs and wishes of husbands to consider. The responsibility for housework is a unilateral one. As itemized by these women such consequences include the wrath of husbands and the ill-health of children' (Oakley 1974:43).

The housewife today is also a consumer and in her cosmic persona is responsible for spending large sums of money. She is therefore a prime target for advertisers. One result of this is that her standards of housekeeping are constant themes of advertisements. On a very obvious level, her children may over-rule her choice by demanding a special brand of food they have seen on television. Certainly, the advertising industry spends much time and money in working out how best to appeal to women.

> 'High turnover products are directed at women. For instance, up to the advent of enzyme powder, "Brand X" was the biggest selling soap powder in Britain. But enzymes were better at removing dirt and when "Brand Y" was introduced it did very well. "Brand X" could not match "Brand Y" in terms of strict efficiency and it started to suffer. What we then set about doing was to look for another property of "Brand X" to advertise. In talking to women one of the things which emerged was worry about rotting the material of clothes. One woman, at a discussion we had, said her husband soaked his paint brushes in "Brand Y" so what we started to stress was that "Brand X" cared for your clothes. Subsequently "Brand Y" slipped right back in the market. This was almost certainly because women are sensible creatures.'
>
> (Advertising executive with J. Walter Thompson)

The advertising industry puts a great deal of pressure on the desire of women to do the best they can for their home and family. It also stresses the convenience and simplicity of many products – surfaces become clean as if by magic, delicious meals only require the unwrapping of the cellophane, children become ecstatic at the sight of hooped spaghetti – it is all made to sound so easy.

It is true that technology has come to the aid of the housewife – Clarence Birdseye, who, in the 1920s was spiritual and actual father of the frozen pea, has indeed made life easier for millions of women. But although technology has removed to some extent the exhausting physical labour of much housework, basically the jobs remain the same. And there is some evidence to suggest that neither housewives nor society think it important to lessen the load. Chancellors of the Exchequer still tax washing machines and refrigerators as luxury items, convenience foods are still expensive.

The ideal of home cooking still has its hold on women – advertisers know this, which no doubt explains the constant references to country goodness and morning fresh products. And even when women have got complicated skills, where for instance, they are good cooks, they often lack the confidence to use them. The cookery editor of *Woman* magazine – which has some six million readers – said that when the magazine produces feature articles on how to entertain people at home, the response from readers is enormous. 'I don't think people are frightened of cooking for their families, but we get loads of queries about having people in – it may be the husband's friends whom she's never met, so advice on timing drinks, what to eat with what, where to serve the coffee and so on goes down very well.' After interviewing twenty prize-winning cooks, *Woman* found that 'a lot of them were frightened to admit they used convenience foods. We were going to see them because they were good home cooks, and home cooking, it's felt, shouldn't include convenience foods. They all admitted using frozen peas, though that isn't a convenience food any more really, but eventually some said they used frozen pastry.'

It is difficult to imagine other craftsmen and craftswomen joiners, painters, engineers, being both unsure about their skills and frightened to admit to using useful tricks of their trade. But then housework today is too often an undervalued, lonely, and unsupported job.

TWO

Education : but for what ?

The education of girls has ever been a matter of great debate. Opinions expressed about it have often been reactionary, sometimes absurd, and occasionally extraordinarily insulting. It comes as no surprise that Dr Johnson said that 'a man is better pleased when he has a good dinner upon his table than when his wife talks Greek'. But it is surprising to find that, nearly a hundred years after Dr Johnson, one of the great Victorian – and radical – educationalists, Miss Dorothea Beale, could ask : 'What seems to be the right means of training girls, so that they may best perform that subordinate part of the world to which I believe they have been called?'

A century or so after Miss Beale, another famous educationalist, and a stirrer-up of hornets' nests, Sir John Newsom, excited both praise and blame with his ideas on the proper education of girls. In 1948, Sir John, then Mr John Newsom, the chief education officer of Hertfordshire, published a short, elegant book: *The Education of Girls*. Sir John has been attacked as being even more reactionary than Dr Johnson. He has also been held responsible for the lack of adventure in subsequent generations of schoolgirls, for their reluctance to touch science subjects, their orientation towards unskilled work after school, and for the promotion of the belief that a job comes second to marriage. He is accused of these sins, not because it is assumed that girls at school are never seen without a copy of his book to hand, but because his views were then enormously influential in planning school curricula, and in forming teachers' views.

The ideas in *The Education of Girls* are representative of their time. After the war there was a longing to get back to some of the old values of peacetime: women as wives and mothers sitting firmly by the fire with a darning needle in one hand and a baby in the other (despite the fact that many had spent the war years doing men's jobs) were essential components of this picture. Newsom, however, did not take a romantic view of the domestic role. He saw it as tough, demanding, and vital to a healthy society. No one would quarrel with this definition today, but more people would dispute the Newsom view that women should be solely responsible for the home and children.

The book, in parts, is enormously sympathetic. 'Heaven knows, we only have to look around us and see what happens to many eager, intelligent and attractive young women after five years of married life – a prospect fit only for the pen of Donne in one of his more bitter moods' (p. 25).

Newsom's solution in 1948 to the problem – as he saw it – of the education of girls was to educate the extremely clever to their full potential. For the next grade down he suggested 'it should not be beyond the wit of woman to devise a course of study for the sixth form, which synthesizes the medieval insistence on skill in housewifery with nineteenth century "accomplishments", and twentieth century emphasis on intellectual training' (p. 117).

For the less clever girls the study of the home and related subjects – English language, physical education, social and political studies and a craft – were Newsom's solutions. He predicted the outraged reactions he indeed got – 'The man raves insanely, away with him'. His reason for foregoing maths, second languages, and science was that he believed it was necessary to do some things well, rather than many things badly.

Thirty years after Newsom, prevailing attitudes towards girls' education have moved away from his philosophy. The social climate has experienced change, but two important factors still set the tone for girls' education: girls' aspirations are largely geared towards marriage; most women are trapped in low-paid jobs. When at the age of sixteen boys are thinking, or being forced to think, about training and a career, girls too often imagine that the wifely role will claim, or rescue, them from employment. This may be reflected in their choice of subjects – substituting 'biology for baton-twirling' as one American educationalist put it. At eighteen, 5 per cent of girls are still at school, compared to 7 per cent of the boys.

The differences in the subjects studied by boys and girls begin, in a modest way, in primary school, where girls may do needlework while boys are being introduced to woodwork. In secondary schools the differences become more marked. In 1972, 138,000 girls sat General Certificate of Education 'O' level exams in home economics, compared with 2,800 boys, while only 300 girls sat exams in woodwork and metalwork, compared with 96,000 boys. In science subjects, more girls studied biology (164,000 entries compared to 88,000 boys examined) while more boys did physics and chemistry – 285,000 boys against 88,000 girls.

Table 1   GCE 'A'-level entries, England and Wales, percentages.

	1962		1972	
	Boys	Girls	Boys	Girls
Percentage of entries				
Arts	25	57	26	54
of which modern languages	7	15	5	13
Science and technical subjects	61	30	49	24
of which mathematics	22	8	18	7
Social science and vocational subjects	14	13	26	22
Total entries (thousands)	184	86	279	188

Source: Statistics of Education

28

The 1972 GCE 'A'-level entries show the same differences of direction, although they also show a growing preference among boys and girls for social science subjects.

But girls seem to have higher pass rates than boys, and to an extent this offsets their lower number of entries.

Table 2   CSE and GCE Summer examinations: entries and results, England and Wales, thousands and percentages.

	1962		1972	
	Boys	Girls	Boys	Girls
Number of entries				
CSE Grade 1			742	608
GCE 'O'-level	1,009	824	1,205	1,100
GCE 'A'-level	184	86	279	188
Results (percentage of entries)				
CSE Grade 1			15	17
GCE 'O'-level pass	57	58	58	63
GCE 'A'-level pass	66	70	68	71

Source: Statistics of Education

This pattern is also seen in Scottish exam results, where in 1972, 70 per cent of the girls who sat Scottish Certificate of Education Higher examinations passed compared to 67 per cent of boys.

Are boys more intelligent than girls? Some generalizations can be made in answer to this apparently absurd question. Most important is that there is an overwhelming similarity between sexes on all levels of human behaviour and functioning. The differences in this context are negligible.

But in certain categories girls do achieve better results than boys while in other categories this is reversed. Girls perform better than boys on verbal tasks, arithmetical tasks, clerical skills, some types of verbal reasoning, rote memory, and fine manual dexterity. Boys perform better on spatial tasks, mathematical problem-solving, mechanical tasks, and on practical abilities. In a recent test on fifteen-year-old school-leavers in Gloucestershire and Hampshire (King 1973; Price 1973) these results were reaffirmed. But, again, what was marked was the considerable degree of overlap of abilities between the sexes. For instance, boys were better at maths, but about 45 per cent of girls scored higher than half the boys. Even in mechanical tasks, where girls are usually considered inept 20–25 per cent of girls scored higher than half the boys.

None of these results, says the *Women and Work: Sex Differences in Society report* (Department of Employment 1974a), really can tell us much. It may be just as much a case of acquired information, interest and motivation, as innate ability. Thus boys who spend, and are encouraged to spend, time playing with Leggo, building blocks, Meccano, and so on are more likely to score higher in 'spatial ability' than girls.

In primary schools, girls do as well as boys – a fact that was reflected in the old eleven plus exam, where success rates were split down the middle between the sexes. Girls, in fact, are generally considered more diligent, and teachers often say that they have a more serious attitude to work. This in itself may be due to conditioning, in that girls are encouraged to be more responsive and more submissive towards authority than boys. In fact, said Douglas, Ross, and Simpson in *All Our Future*, written in the days of the eleven plus, a larger proportion of girls than boys would have 'benefited' from a grammar school education. With adolescence, secondary school boys start to catch up and then overtake the girls. Yet those girls who do take 'O' levels beat the boys: 23 per cent of girl school leavers in one age group leave with five or more 'O' levels compared to 22·5 per cent of boys. Two years later, the girls have fallen behind: 6·6 per cent of girls leave with three or more 'A' levels compared to 9·1 per cent of boys (DES statistics, 1972). What pressures and conditions account for this drop-out rate? Who or what should be taken to task?

Discrimination begins in the home. If none of us experienced the overt discouragement of the Victorian who declared 'Knowing the multiplication tables will be of no use to my daughter in a drawing room, so why should she bother to learn it' (and no doubt she never did), plenty of other pressures are at work. The hand that rocked the cradle still rocks the cradle. It is a model of womanhood that no girl can escape. A working-class housewife, interviewed by Ann Oakley (1974) commented that her daughter was growing into the same mould as herself. 'She's got a cot, and dolls, and now she's got a pram ... and it's all miniatures of what you have in real life later on ... I don't think that's right ... and I think I'd rather buy her trains and motor cars.'

Betty Friedan, author of *The Feminine Mystique* laid some pertinent cards on the table. Talking to college girls in the late 1950s she observed that of those who were not in an obsessive hurry to 'get a man' and who had broader-based interests, almost all had mothers or images of women committed to wider horizons than home and family. 'My mother happens to be a teacher' was one comment, and 'My best friend's mother is a doctor; she always seems so busy and happy'. Fathers, too, bear a responsibility. Ms Sheila Wood, Secretary of the Association of Assistant Mistresses in Secondary Schools, maintains that the image the father has of his daughter will dictate her endeavours. It is not surprising then that, despite the widening of women's educational horizons over the last hundred years, girls still lag behind in educational achievement.

Women students at one college of education – all of whom had left school early and were busy catching up on their education – said that their marriage expectations had been considered of primary importance and that neither they nor their parents had thought of them as marketable in any other capacity. They were not a 'good investment'.

This attitude is not the doubtful privilege of the working classes. Middle-class parents who choose to pay for their children's education are also looking for a return from their economic investment. And returns, in traditional bourgeois society too, come from the men. Middle-class boys are sent off to their private schools – often crippling their parents financially on the way. Meanwhile their sisters, who might possibly be the bright ones of the family, go to, for example, the local convent where, devotions do not necessarily lead to scholarship. Indeed, parents of all classes are generally less discerning about the academic achievements at their daughters' schools than their sons'. A study made by a Norwegian sociologist found that 40 per cent of parents thought that an education was more important for a boy than for a girl (quoted in Turner 1974).

Parents tend to send their daughters to fee-paying schools for social not academic reasons. An echo of Victoriana. 'Time was', said Miss Buss at her school's first speech day in 1850 'when a very little reading, less writing, plain work, pudding making and pickling constituted the amount of education of a girl in the middle classes.'

Single-sex schools have often, somewhat unfairly, been accused of perpetuating the secondary role of women in society. One out of every three girls in England and Wales goes to a single-sex school (only 10 per cent in Scotland). The traditional weakness of girls in maths and science (nearly twice as many boys as girls get three science 'A' levels) is sometimes attributed to the inadequacy of science teaching in all-girls schools. For example, in co-educational schools, says Douglas Pidgeon (1970), girls achieve greater success in maths than in single-sex schools. 'Where girls are taught in an atmosphere where the traditional female suspicion of maths is less noticeable and where, perhaps, the teachers are less inclined to doubt their abilities in the subject, then they make greater strides than they would otherwise have done' (quoted in Turner 1974).

Women science teachers in all girls' schools are in short supply although men do fill the gaps in the science departments. Scientific equipment is often inadequate. A Ministry of Education Bulletin in 1956 actually recommended less space for laboratories in girls' schools than boys'. None of these factors will foster the impetus required for girls to concentrate on physics and forget the Eng. Lit. It requires a fair degree of interest to walk twenty-five minutes to the local boys' school to join a science class. One sixth former at an Islington girls' comprehensive said: 'I'm the only one doing biology, just me and the teacher in the class, and I haven't the faintest idea what standard I should be at. I need competition, especially from boys in a mixed sixth form. The boys hate girls being good at science so you have to try and beat them.'

Yet official reports suggest that mixed schools are not instrumental in breaking down traditional barriers. What tends to happen is that the established pattern of girls for the arts and boys for the sciences is more marked in mixed schools. 'Girls are more likely to choose a science and boys a language in a single-sex school than they are in a mixed school, though in a mixed school a higher percentage of pupils may be offered these subjects' (Department of Education and Science 1975).

Sheila Wood bases her case for single-sex schools on the effects of boy/girl relations during adolescence.

'It is a fact that single-sex schools keep the girls in longer. In today's climate girls are not ready to be competitive with boys. They think they'll love it, but brains and sexual attraction do not seem to go together. Girls are anxious creatures and terrified of failure. Our society is just not ready for co-education; "positive" discrimination must remain for the time being.'

One Leeds grammar school headmistress also supported this argument (quoted in *Locked up Daughters*). 'In a masculine dominated society,' she said, 'the girls will opt for the obviously feminine role – the non-academic early-leaver. The advantages gained from having as heads of department brilliant men, especially in science, may be taken by a few, but the mass will go for popularity with the boys by not competing.' An American survey of women students reported that 40 per cent of them downgraded their academic ability in front of their male contemporaries (Turner 1974).

But we no longer live in times when women can afford or aspire to a lifetime of pure housewifery. When Newsom's *The Education of Girls* was written (1948) the proportion of women between the ages of fifteen and twenty-nine staying at home to their sisters working outside the home was 13 to 5. The conventional wisdom after the last war was that leisure would increase and that this would greatly affect women, more and more of whom would stay at home. (The fact that working in the home rarely qualifies as leisure is nowadays less often ignored than it used to be.) In fact the reverse has happened. Over 40 per cent of married women now go out to work. Indeed, the percentage of married women who work outside the home has doubled since 1951. There is no indication that the pendulum will swing back. The object now should be to alter the attitudes women have about themselves, when they are in a position to make choices about the kind of work they will do. And the only time they are in this position is at school.

At the beginning of 1975 Ernest Armstrong, then Minister of State at the Department of Education and Science, said that a campaign was necessary to persuade women to grasp the opportunities opening up to them to take higher qualifications. Far too many women, he said, wrote themselves off well below their potential. Yet one of the organizations responsible for the lack of career consciousness in schoolgirls, and for the reluctance of women to stretch their capacities in traditionally male subjects, is the Department of Education and Science. Indeed, it was itself severely reprimanded by the Select Committee on the Anti-Discrimination Bill in 1973 for not being aware of the problem of inequality between boys and girls at school. A DES booklet entitled *Careers Education in Secondary Schools*, published in 1973, does not once mention the problem of encouraging girls in a career, nor does it discuss how girls can be started off on a wider range of subjects than the usual arts/social science/commercial axis. Admittedly, the budgets allocated in schools to careers guidance and discussion were appalling – only 2 per cent of schools spent over £150 a year on it for pupils of both sexes – but the DES has failed lamentably in the past to tackle the problem of the schoolgirl being inexorably pushed towards the dead-end job.

The best of advice at one time, may become oddly out of date a few years later. Ruth Miller's book *Careers for Girls* was first published in 1966 and was the first guide of its kind. It is extensively used by careers advisers and its coverage of over 300 careers is impressive and thorough. But the book does not take a feminist view. In the section on a career in broadcasting it advises, 'A good way to start is as a well trained secretary. Any secretarial job is worth taking.' The chances are, sadly, that a well-trained secretary who wants to get into broadcasting will become a well-trained secretary who has accepted that she will never get into broadcasting.

Schools cannot, through the mere presence of a feminist careers teacher and a selection of pictures showing girls in hard hats welding pipe lines, change the conventional attitudes of girls and parents. However, a school is often the only place where girls can be given a choice and where, on the simplest level, they can be given information about the kind of jobs available. There is a great deal of evidence that this kind of information and discussion is lacking in our schools.

In a survey commissioned by the Department of Education and Science and undertaken by Lancaster University into the reasons for the recent slackening of demand for higher education places, the report on 1,000 fifth formers found that one third of boys and 44 per cent of girls felt they had not received enough advice or information on their futures. Many of the comments lamented the dearth of lectures on various occupations, and the lack of full-time careers teachers. The same survey listed the attributes that fifth formers look for in employment.

34

The emphasis that the girls interviewed in this survey put on training, promotion, and enjoyment of a job, contrasts sadly with the dull, routine work most school-leavers end up with. 'Getting a good training on the job' was considered very important by 65·9 per cent of the girls (73·4 per cent of boys), while only 5·1 per cent of girls did not consider this important. Other features of jobs that girls believed to be important were 'people to work with' (86·1 per cent) – boys also felt this to be important; enjoyable work (girls 79·9 per cent and boys 80·1 per cent) and good chance of promotion (68·7 per cent for girls and 69 per cent for boys). These sort of figures suggest that girls do think seriously about their future, and that their potential is not being fully exploited (*Times Educational Supplement*, 12 March, 1976).

A group of sixteen- and seventeen-year-old girls in a South London comprehensive were asked by the authors in 1975 what they thought of the careers guidance in their school. These were girls who had all chosen to stay on at school and whose parents were keen for them to study. But none of them had been encouraged by the school to be ambitious. They had been told, they said, by the careers master that the two careers for girls were nursing and clerical work. Another teacher had told them : 'There are too many girls wasting their time in education when they could be earning good money in Woolworth's.'

One girl who was interested in journalism had been told 'that's not the kind of thing girls want to do'. Another girl, studying for 'A' levels had admitted to the careers teacher that she was taking typing as a standby. 'Well', said he, 'I'll get you some leaflets on the post office and the bank.' The girls wanted to be encouraged 'to be equal with the boys'. The teacher's attitude seemed to them to be, 'You can't do men's jobs, so don't bother trying.'

In the more academic girls' schools the traps are different. There can be a concentration on getting bright girls into university without pointing out to them the possible careers thereafter. This leads directly to the 'over qualified secretary' – the woman who has a degree in a non-vocational subject like English and finds it hard to fit it to a job. It also leads to a neglect of the futures of girls who are not aiming for a university education. In *English Girls' Boarding Schools* Mallory Wober found that girls held the somewhat vague ambition of being 'good at work'

35

above all others. The girls he interviewed told him they thought a greater emphasis should be given to careers. One said 'Everyone here applies for university without any idea of what career they will follow once they have left there' (p. 91).

A group of young women at the London College for the Distributive Trades told us that because of bad or non-existent careers guidance at school they had arrived at the College more through luck than design. One girl, who had been at a grammar school, said, 'If you didn't go to university it meant you were thick, in their eyes, and you landed in the mud and had to pull yourself out and find something on your own. A lot of girls just ended up in jobs their parents thought were good for them – like secretarial.' Another girl had been presented only with the choices of teaching or nursing in seven different talks with different teachers. The point is not that girls should not want to get married, nor that they should be trained to ignore the responsibilities of children which they mostly, quite correctly, believe they will have. But schools have not yet caught up with the fact that 'the average woman' will marry, have children, and be employed – all in one life.

In *Patriarchal Attitudes* (1972) Eva Figes includes excerpts from essays written in 1968 by a group of fourteen- and fifteen-year-old girls at a London grammar school on the subject 'Today is my 80th birthday and I look back on the time when I left high school'. Although most of the girls wanted some sort of further education they did not envisage working for more than a year after training. Marriage would thereafter call them to higher duties. They might, most said, take some sort of part-time job when their children started school, but by the age of forty-five they would become housewives again. In all they looked back, from their eightieth year, on about ten years of employment in their lives. Their basic assumption, one which is fostered by society as a whole, Ms Figes commented, was that 'housework and the care of a man and children is a woman's work and duty ... and that any other interests she may have must be curtailed by the demands that these duties make on her' (p. 185).

But girls in school also need models. They need to see proof among their teachers that women are not necessarily confined to secondary roles; that they can have satisfactory personal lives (though for many girls this may mean simply having a a husband) as well as holding down responsible and senior jobs. A report by the Association of Assistant Mistresses (1976) showed how often women teachers are not aware of the potential of this missionary role. At one conference of the association a survey showed that there was a dearth of applications from women for headships of schools and of departments. A fear of prejudice was found, which, the report said, may not always be well founded.

> 'Statistics showed that men were far more persistent than women in making applications and were ready to make as many as a hundred for a level of post they were seeking. Few women applied for more than three or four posts at a particular level. They seemed to believe that rejection implied a judgment that they were not suited for promotion.'
>
> (AAM 1976:7)

In 1974–5 male students at universities outnumbered women in a ratio of nearly 2–1, although this disproportion had greatly narrowed in the years from 1962, when only 25 per cent of students at universities were women. Language and literature courses, studied by over one-third of women students, were most popular, followed by social, administrative, and business studies courses. Science subjects came next with architecture, engineering, and technological courses coming at the bottom of the list of subjects in which women students are found. One lone girl was admitted, between 1969–73, to study mining. The courses chosen by men were almost the reverse of those studied by women with science heading the list, engineering coming next, and arts subjects at the bottom.

In further education – defined by the Department of Education and Science as everything studied after school excluding university and polytechnic degree courses – women actually dominate but, predictably enough, they congregate in either traditional female subjects or in non-vocational courses. Half the men attending further education establishments in 1972 were doing so in day-release classes but compared with these half a million men, only 100,000 women were to be found in day release. Over a million women went to classes in the evenings compared to half a million men. Women also predominate in colleges of education

The fact that a woman has gone into full-time further education or training does not mean that she escapes the sprung trap of tradition. Those few girls (5 per cent of girl school leavers in 1973) who took apprenticeships were mostly found in hairdressing. Over a third went into clerical work, from which there is often no exit to more demanding or fulfilling work.

But there are portents that indicate change. A careers adviser at the Polytechnic of Central London said that though women do predictable courses, and though a man will work from the premises that he will have a job and a girl will say something like, 'I'm engaged, my fiance is in Nottingham, what can I do in Nottingham?', women are becoming more aware that they will need something to return to once families are older, mortgages are partly paid, and thirty years of working life stretches ahead.

But these women still have to battle with attitudes other than their own. A report from the Standing Conference of University Appointments Services published in 1975 commented that services in the North East, Scotland, and Northern Ireland had noted entrenched male thinking in their areas, commonly reflected in women's attitudes too. 'Many of our women are under-achievers in that they accept the role that many Scottish men seemed to suggest was the suitable one for them as ladies.' Those who wished to break down barriers were often destined for a rough time with local employers, the report said. The attitudes as well as the subjects learnt by girls in schools, and in further education, largely determine where they will spend the rest of their working lives. The fact that so many women find themselves in dull, badly-paid jobs without prospect of advance reflects the failure of the education system to exploit the full potential of half the population.

THREE

Low pay : an aptitude for dull, repetitive work

'Women's employment has continued to be concentrated in a small number of industries and confined to a range of jobs which might be described as "women's work". Even where women work alongside men, they usually hold positions of lower responsibility and perform tasks of a less skilled nature ... men are the employers, managers, top professionals, foremen and skilled workers in our society.'

(*Social Trends* 1974 : 16)

Most employed women in Britain are doing a job that provides a background against which other people can carry out what society believes are the more productive and important kinds of work. The woman employed outside her home is much more likely to be making biscuits than cars, serving coffee than building ships, doing the dry cleaning rather than the dock work.

With few exceptions, most women earn far less than most men. Men have always been considered the breadwinners, which has meant that – in terms of cash, training, and promotion – employers have rarely taken women's work as seriously as men's. Neither, until recently, have many unions.

Men and women rarely do the same jobs. The major differences are that women are concentrated in a small number of trades and industries, that they are earning – even with the Equal Pay Act – about half as much as men do, and that part-time work is almost wholly done by women. (Just over a third of women workers in this country are employed part time.) The other difference, which springs from these three factors, is that women workers are mainly unskilled, and the number of skilled women is in fact decreasing.

The decrease in the proportion of skilled women workers provides a depressing example of how women have inherited a growing share of the unskilled work in an industrial society. Official figures reinforce this trend since many women's jobs are considered, often unfairly, as unskilled or semi-skilled whatever the true nature of the work – a reflection on the lowly status bestowed on much of women's work. In 1911 just under a third of all manual workers were women – today the proportion remains roughly the same. But while in 1911 24 per cent of these women workers were skilled, now the figure stands at only 14 per cent, while the percentage of unskilled women has almost doubled from 15 per cent then, to 27 per cent today (Department of Employment 1974).

In 1977 nearly nine million women work outside their homes (the Department of Employment's choice phrase is 'economically active') – a striking increase of more than one million on the 1961 figures. Of this total, more than half worked in three service industries: the distributive trades (shops, mail order, warehouses) accounted for 17 per cent of the female workforce; professional and scientific (typists, technicians, secretaries, teachers, and nurses) 23 per cent; and miscellaneous services (laundries, catering, dry cleaners, hairdressers), 12 per cent.

In manufacturing, women are similarly concentrated. A quarter of all women working outside the home are employed in manufacturing industries (1975 figures), and of these half are in only four industries: food and drink manufacture, clothing and footwear, textiles, electrical engineering.

This concentration is not found in male employment – no single industry employed more than 10 per cent of the male work force in 1971. The five sections (the Department of Employment lists 27, into which are classified all major economic groups from agriculture to defence), where women employees outnumber men, are:

clothing and footwear manufacture	74 per cent women
distributive trades	56 per cent women
insurance, banking, finance and business	52 per cent women
miscellaneous services	55 per cent women
professional and scientific services	67 per cent women

All these groups, except for insurance and banking, employ a lot of part-time labour and most of the women working in them are either in the lowest paying ranks, or at the bottom of the middle paying grades. In April 1976, for example, the average hourly earnings of women manual workers in jobs in miscellaneous services (catering, hairdressing and so on) were the lowest of all industry groups. Next came the distributive trades, then jobs in clothing and footwear, and after that textiles (Department of Employment 1975: Table 56).

The assumption is often made that women work for pin money, that what they earn is somehow less important than that earned by a man. A warehouse supervisor in a Bolton textile factory said that this attitude is common among women themselves. 'They say, "If there's any overtime going the men should have it".' The supervisor thought this attitude was wrong, but that it was often expressed, even by women on their own. And it is true that women – partly because of legislation and partly because of family, do much less overtime than men. In 1973 overtime earnings accounted for 16 per cent of the earnings of male manual workers and only 3 per cent of the earnings of full-time women manual workers (Department of Employment 1974).

The proportion of married women working outside the home has increased dramatically since the last war. Since 1961 the increase in the female labour force has been made up of married women, with the number of single women employed actually falling (from 3,808,000 in 1961 to 3,248,000 in 1971). At the last count 42 per cent of married women were employed outside the home, and married women composed 62 per cent of the female workforce.

> 'It is evident that the community is already extremely dependent upon married women to maintain, let alone increase, our gross national product, and it seems that this dependence is going to increase. It is evident too, that a growing number of families are to a considerable degree dependent upon the mother's earnings.' (Mepham 1974:32)

But because most women workers are responsible for families, the work they look for outside the home is the sort that requires little or no training because family commitments in time and cash do not allow for training, will be either part-time or outside normal working hours, and will be quite near home. These factors neatly add up to the main components of a low-paid job. The now defunct National Prices and Incomes Board asked women working part-time in cleaning and NHS ancillary jobs why they worked part-time. The most important reason for taking a part-time job was, 'its working hours followed closely by the type of work offered and its nearness to their homes. Good pay was low on the list of priorities and the training offered (if any) was hardly rated at all. The overriding reason for not working full-time ... was home and family.' (NPIB 1971).

The statistics produced by the Department of Employment show that the hours worked by women bear a close relationship to the age and number of their dependent children. In 1971, 58 per cent of married women without dependent children (children still at school) worked more than thirty hours a week but only 30 per cent of those with two dependent children did this. On the other hand, there is some evidence that women with more than four children tend to work longer hours, presumably because of a greater need for money. Thus, according to a sample taken from the 1971 census, 16 per cent of mothers with four or more children worked more than thirty-six hours a week, more than double the proportion who worked between thirty and thirty-six hours a week.

By June 1975 there were 4,248,000 part-time employees of whom 3,551,000 were women. 'The Department's forecasts indicate that the major part of the potential growth in the labour supply over the next few years is likely to consist of women who are looking for part-time rather than full-time employment.' (*Women and Work*. Department of Employment *Gazette*. January 1975).

Part-time work is a pernicious barrier to women's equality with men. The jobs where part-timers are traditionally most welcome are in catering, cleaning, laundering, the food and drink industries, shops, the National Health Service, and some offices. And these jobs are, not surprisingly, familiar extensions to women's domestic work.

In retailing, where a third of all part-time women workers are employed, it has been suggested (Robinson and Wallace 1973) that part-time work pulls down wage rates by keeping them at the statutory or agreed minimum. And the International Labour Organization has launched a number of hefty criticisms. 'Part-time employment enables employers to refuse vocational training for women ... it avoids all the problems concerning care of children, welfare for mothers ... it masks unemployment because part-timers are regarded as being on full-time' (Income Data Services 1973).

One of the major effects of part-time work is that it acts as a further brake on women being trained or promoted. In 1973, the Office of Population, Censuses, and Surveys found that women part-timers were eligible for promotion in less than one-fifth of firms surveyed, and had training opportunities in only one-quarter. 'Although the availability of part-time employment is increasing most such work is still undemanding, ill-paid and of low status with no prospects of advancement. Many of those who want a "decent job" are forced to work more hours than they would wish, resulting in a tension between home and work responsibilities' (Department of Employment 1974a).

The opportunities that could exist in part-time work for women (see Chapter 4 on civil service proposals for greater use of part-time work in administrative and senior jobs) have not, on the whole, been taken up by firms. The fact that most managers of businesses have but a hazy idea of what family responsibilities their employees have (how many married women are employed, for instance) suggests that hours worked are rarely laid down with the convenience of employees in mind. Too often a firm will announce that it has a shift system to suit its women workers, without being aware that one end of the shift may fall at as inconvenient a time as either end of a nine to five day.

'A finding from the present survey is that ... very many im-plementers are ignorant of the extent of the family respon-sibilities of the women who work at their establishments. It probably follows that they cannot be fully aware of the possible effects of personnel policy on the well-being of female employees. Thus they would be unlikely to be able to esti-mate, for example, the magnitude of the possible demand for child care facilities at the work place.'   (Hunt 1975:111)

Most women appear remarkably tolerant of the dreary and repetitive work many of them have to do. 'The best job I've ever had', was how one woman on the assembly line of an Edinburgh bakery factory described her job. What she did was this. She took eight shortbread fingers off the large metal tray which carried them from the oven and placed them in a narrow con-veyor belt which deposited them on a cellophane wrapping machine. She was doing what is known as a 'simple repetitive task' – deadening, monotonous, and badly paid. But it was far preferable to other jobs in the factory because it was away from the noise and heat of the machinery in the baking section.

The baking industry in Scotland was one of the industries re-ferred to the Industrial Arbitration Board by the Department of Employment in 1975 because of the lack of progress towards equal pay. 'Women have been employed for years in baking as cheap labour', said George Currie of the Scottish Baking Union. 'They were brought in in the 1920s to do jobs that men once did.' The industry's practices reflect many of the habits that im-prison women in the menial, badly paid, and poorly thought of jobs, for the most part working with other women who share the same consciousness, and the same timidity about their potential.

In the Scottish baking industry, for instance, women are not allowed to work in fermentation, that is, with yeast in the early stages of bread production. Like other bans imposed on where women can work, it is a hang-over from the days when con-siderable strength was needed to handle the flour, to make the dough, and to process it – all done by hand. To exclude women now from these jobs is to exclude them from the higher paid jobs. So they work in other areas of production – either preparing scones, shortbread, cakes, cake decorations or cleaning and greasing tins and doing packing and dispatch.

On the assembly lines, Edinburgh women in 1975 were working beside men earning a fifth as much again as themselves. One middle aged woman said: 'The women put the meat and the onions into the pies and the men put the potatoes on top and for working with onions instead of potatoes the women get 82 per cent of the male rate.' The women resented this, and an added insult was the daily hiring of casual male workers who were paid more than long-serving members of the female work force. The arbitrary nature of the division of labour between the sexes is of considerable concern to the baking union. There appears to be no logic about the ban on women doing jobs that are either too hot, heavy, or harmful. In one bakery it was the woman's job to take the newly baked bread out of the ovens and put it on the racks. In another this was designated a man's job.

Although in manufacturing as a whole the wages for women are higher than they are for their sisters in shops, canteens, and restaurants, where the majority of workers in an industry are women, the wage levels are pulled down. Thus textiles, clothing, and footwear were the three lowest paid manufacturing industries in April 1975 (Department of Employment 1976:Table 56).

Average gross weekly earnings for full-time manual men and women, April 1976:

	women	men
food, drink, and tobacco	£39·3	£64·9
chemicals and allied industries	£39·4	£67·0
mechanical engineering	£41·6	£64·3
electrical engineering	£41·2	£62·5
textiles	£36·3	£58·8
clothing and footwear	£32·6	£52·1
bricks, pottery, glass, cement etc	£39·2	£66·0
papers, printing, and publishing	£40·4	£69·0
other manufacturing industries	£37·3	£63·2
transport and communication	£50·8	£68·8
distributive trades	£32·8	£53·1
professional and scientific services	£39·0	£56·4
miscellaneous services	£33·3	£50·2
public administration	£42·7	£54·7

(Department of Employment 1976: Tables 54, 56)

The textile industry employs 155,000 women out of 280,000

workers and these numbers are contracting yearly. Increasing capital investment in the industry, which brings with it more automation and more technology – has further squeezed women out of the skilled or highly paid jobs. At one time it seemed that technology would aid women – as well as men – by removing the need for physical strength from many jobs. In textile manufacture the more modern factories have indeed replaced human strength with electric power, but the opportunity for breaking through the craft barrier has not been taken by women or their representatives.

Miss Hilda Unsworth, Secretary of the Bolton Weavers Association, says that the main reason for women losing their hold on the skilled job of weaving is that the expenditure on the new plant requires factories to have continuous twenty-four hour working. And protective legislation forbids the employment of most women after 8 p.m. 'There are a lot of men coming into the industry now with the new machinery. There's one mill in Bolton that has 24 hour working, seven days a week and it's all men.'

Among the weavers equal pay has existed for many years. Rates in one new factory weaving covers for continental quilts were around £48 a week for men and women in the middle of 1975. This was for shift work which included shift allowances. At this factory there are fifteen women weavers on the day shifts tending 252 machines. Since the factory opened in 1972 the demands of a three and a half million pound plant have led to twenty-four hour working and to the firm taking on boys rather than girls as trainee weavers. The training supervisor for weaving, Mrs Joan Lees, said 'I think women in the future will be helping the men and not doing the weaving themselves. Our big grumble here is that we have no promotion for women. As a training instructor I'm the most promoted person here. There are no women supervisors. The managing director said to me if it comes about that this is an all male factory it'll be because sixty machines have to be looked after at a time – but women could do that. But in the future they may want seven-day working too, and women can't work on Sundays or at nights.'

The difficulty for women weavers, says Miss Unsworth, is that they do not want to work extended shifts. They find family responsibilities difficult enough to fit in with their present working hours. But this, inevitably, means that women will lose some of the good, skilled jobs they have managed to hold until now. The problems and ambiguities of protective legislation – which lays down certain conditions about hours and times where women are employed – are discussed in a later chapter, but women weavers are conscious that if they lost place to men in this skilled and relatively well paid job the alternatives are few. 'We had a factory closed in Bolton last year and, do you know, I found six of those skilled women weavers working as domestics in the infirmary, I was shaken, I can tell you. But they said to me they were quite happy. They said it wasn't as bad as I might have thought.'

This flexibility among women workers is well known, and it is something not shared to the same extent by male workers. Women will slide from industry to industry at different points in their lives, and while this mobility gives certain advantages – a wider range of jobs (even if these are mainly unskilled) and a certain appeal to employers – it also means that women are less likely than men to think of staying in one industry and acquiring skills. It also affects their interest in joining a union.

The position of women does not seem to improve even in those trades and industries that are changing, that are new or where labour is so short that it might be imagined that women would be valued as precious gold. In the clothing industry 80 per cent of the 360,000 employees are women, and with the footwear industry, it employs the largest proportion of girls leaving school. Clothing industry employees decline in numbers by about 2 per cent a year and one of the great worries of the employers (there are about 7,000 firms in the industry, many of them employing below thirty people) is the vast turnover of labour, which runs at 50 per cent a year.

The structure of the clothing industry means that chances of promotion are slim for women workers, because there is nowhere for them to be promoted to. Often factory grades will only consist of machinists and managers, with sometimes a supervisor in between. Many of the women may not welcome responsibility because of home commitments, although they are aware of the dead-end nature of a machinist's job. The Clothing and Allied Products Industry Training Board says that one reason for labour shortage in a city like Leeds is that mothers, who themselves work in the clothing industry, 'hit the roof' if it is suggested that their daughters might follow them into it. And a Board bulletin in 1975 to employers said: 'Our failure has always been one of keeping employees when we have recruited them. Everything is blamed, from the welfare state to promiscuous sailors, but this cannot release the manager from his responsibility ... It is often found that factories with severe labour turnover problems are within short walking distance of other factories with no labour turnover problems.'

More cogently the bulletin pointed out that often wages in the industry were as much as 12p an hour below the average manufacturing wage of 58.4p (October 1973, Department of Employment *Gazette*) and that the manufacture of lingerie, hats, caps, dresses, and shirts, where proportions of women are highest was particularly poorly paid (7–12p below the average), whereas rates in outerwear and rainwear, where more men are employed, were only 3.5p below.

Flexible working time is often not considered possible in clothing manufacture because of sectionalized factory lines – one woman doing the collars for dresses while others do sleeves, belts, and skirts – and about 20 per cent of the labour force works part time. But a report by the Clothing Economic Development Council (1972) on what women workers thought of their industry, and the recommendations drawn from the results of questionnaires, is revealing: 'Try to involve the girls (sic) in decisions like flexibility of hours and holidays, smoking and eating facilities....' the report advises. 'If possible hold regular meetings to discuss their problems and explain yours....'

The report advises employers to ask themselves certain questions in the complex endeavour of finding out how to keep staff. 'Are the working conditions reasonable for a woman? WOULD YOU USE THEIR TOILETS?' (their capitals).

The report said that supervisors got far more satisfaction from their jobs than did machinists.

> 'Packers, folders and pressers have less commitment to their job, more would stay at home if they could and they care less about the type of work they do ... Of people leaving 43 per cent agreed that only a cabbage could get satisfaction from the job. Well over half find their job boring and repetitive, though 60 per cent found the atmosphere friendly.'
> (Clothing Economic Development Council 1972)

Just over a tenth of all women workers labour in the jobs

which come under the collective title of the service industries. These million women do the work which is similar to the work they do at home – cooking, cleaning (especially cleaning), serving up the food, getting a place nice. The number of women who clean for a living is unknown because, of all the work women do outside the home, this is the area where they are most isolated, least regarded, and among the least organized in union terms. But cleaning is also a growth industry. The Contract Cleaning and Maintenance Association, which represents 300 members, claims that the industry is growing by between 10 and 15 per cent a year. 'People are more and more putting out their cleaning work to specialists because that relieves them of the whole chore of hiring and firing.' One cleaning combine, Pritchards, the largest in Britain, has a turnover of £325 million annually and operates in South Africa, Portugal, and the Gulf States as well as Britain.

Cleaners are being recruited by unions like the National Union of Public Employees (NUPE) and the Civil Service Union, but they are not easy to reach, and many of them have never thought of the work they do as meriting the attention of a union. Mrs Ann Meek is the chargehand among the cleaners at a London University college. With four other women she cleans the maths building of the college for 54p an hour (July 1975). She said that she had to bully about 25 other cleaners into joining NUPE to get a decent wage – the preceding Christmas the cleaners had received a princely rise of fourpence an hour.

'If you ask for a rise they say why don't you go and work at the hospital or at the school for the dinners. But I like the job, why should I give it up? I've been here since the building was put up, that was 12 years ago, and I don't want to move. Though when they built the building they never thought of the cleaners, all these stairs, lifts that don't work, no room for cleaners to leave things.'

The cleaners in the college thought it would have been preferable to be employed directly by the college rather than by the contract cleaning firm. They would then, they believed, have had more chance of getting cost of living rises and London allowances.

Cleaning is not, in itself, a pleasant or desirable job. Most cleaners are in the job because the work is near their homes, takes place either in the early morning or in the evening when young children are asleep or can be minded by somebody else. While there is a satisfaction in leaving a place shining and neat, there is no joy in cleaning up real filth. 'The students can be filthy, really it would make you ill. The toilets and the union after parties are terrible, you'd never credit the mess that we have to clear up' (Mrs Meek).

The Civil Service Union, whose 6,000 cleaning members are almost all employed by the Civil Service believe that more and more young women are becoming cleaners in order to supplement the family income. The work itself is changing.

'Cleaning is becoming increasingly a capital intensive industry, which is shattering when you consider that it's based on the work of women. You now get charged heads on mops and dusters which suck in the dust automatically, and if you explain these machines to a woman who has been a cleaner all her life and you tell her that she has been, in effect, doing it all wrong for years, that the way she was doing it was not scientifically correct, then it's hard for her. After all, that's the way she cleans her own home.' (Civil Service Union official)

Cleaning is, as a result of its transformation into a capital intensive industry, also separating the woman, in many large buildings, from the result of her work. Productivity schemes where one woman does the floor cleaning, another empties the waste paper baskets, another polishes up, may be efficient but they also deny anyone the satisfaction of the finished job: 'Leaving Mr Smith's room lovely for him may not be much of a satisfaction but if it is the only one available it seems a pity to reorganize it out of existence' (Civil Service Union official).

Just under 10 per cent of the country's labour force is covered by Wages Councils. And one reason why many women are in badly paid jobs is that a quarter of all employed women work in industries and trades covered by a Wages Council. The forty-five councils set minimum wage rates for their industries and also have powers of inspection through the Department of Employment to see that these rates are being paid. Many more women than men are covered by wages councils. Thus hotel and catering (55 per cent of employees are women), retail and distribution (56 per cent of all employees are women), the clothing trades (74 per cent of employees are women), as well as hairdressing and laundries, all fall under Wages Councils.

Wages Council industries are among the lowest paid out of all the twenty-six industrial groupings of work. Indeed, that was the reason for setting them up. In 1909 the Trade Boards, predecessors of the Wages Councils, were formed as a means of raising wages in the sweated trades (box making, tailoring, and chain making were the first three trades to be tackled). The Low Pay Unit, which has concentrated on investigating industries covered by Wages Councils, is scathing about their deficiencies. The Unit says that the Wages Councils have a dismal record over the past thirty years in raising the pay of the worst off sections of the community. There are 2,200,000 women covered by Wages Council agreements. About a third of these earned less (in April 1974) than £17 a week.

It is easy to see why the Wages Councils are unpopular with those concerned about low pay. The Councils consist of representatives of the employers of the particular trade, the workers' representatives, and three independent members. They set a rate that becomes the statutory minimum rate for the job and which must be paid. Failure to pay the rate incurs a fine of up to £100 for the erring employers. But it is extremely easy for the employer, either out of ignorance or ill will, to pay less than he or she should. The wages inspectorate of the Department of Employment found in 1975 that a staggering 30 per cent of firms visited were paying less than the statutory minimum rate. The now deceased Commision of Industrial Relations found that only 5 per cent of workers covered by a Wages Council knew of its existence, far less what its functions were. The Wages Councils themselves are not forthcoming with information, and appear to dislike even the most watery glimmer of publicity.

Wages Councils cover very small firms. The average number of workers in firms in the Wages Council sector is seven. The average number of employees in firms covered by the retail distribution Wages Councils is 4.9, and in hotels and catering the figure is 8.4. In small businesses, unions are, almost by definition, not strong and out of 1.2 million hotel and catering workers only about 50,000 are unionized.

Wages Councils also cover very tiny numbers of workers in certain industries. The tradition of the sweated trades still lingers on. There are 650 women in the ostrich fancy feather and artificial flower industry, 6,000 women in the linen and cotton handkerchief industry, 14,000 in the pin, hook and eye business, 4,000 in the fur industry, 6,000 in hat, cap and millinery, and 2,500 in the sack and bag industry.

The complexity of the Wages Councils regulations and pay structure would defy the keenest intelligence. There are four Wages Councils covering for instance, the hotel, catering, and bar industry. The Licensed Residential and Licensed Restaurant Wages Council, the largest of the councils, which covers 390,000 workers (Brown and Winyard 1975) lists sixty-four different occupations, with twenty-one different statutory minimum rates. Additionally, the rates will vary in different parts of the country. All this makes it very difficult for people in hotel and catering to know exactly how much they should be paid. The true rates, anyway, are low. Waitresses covered by this Council, for example, had a rate agreed for them in October 1974 of £13·47p for a forty hour week.

The hotel and catering industry, which employs 11 per cent of all women workers, is popular with women for a number of reasons. There is a lot of part-time work. Traditionally, for the woman who had no family responsibilities and was not married, the work was also convenient because it often provided live-in accommodation. Then the work is, after all, doing what is supposed to come naturally. Also in women's 'favour' is the fact that the work requires no training, because skills are picked up as the work is done.

In 1974 a quarter of full-time women workers in hotels and catering were paid less than 50p an hour. Of the million or so women working both full and part-time in the industry 90 per cent earned less than the TUC minimum wage of £30 a week (Brown and Winyard 1975).

The 1971 figures from the Department of Employment show where women worked in the catering industry: 79,000 waitresses; 22,000 restaurateurs; 117,000 cooks; 98,000 kitchen hands; 70,000 barmaids; 417,000 maids, valets, and related service workers; 289,000 canteen assistants and counter hands. Catering may be thought to be ideal women's work, but women do not think much of it. They vote with their feet, and the hotel and catering industry has an annual 50 per cent staff turnover. High turnover and high absenteeism rates are often associated with women workers. But there is some evidence to suggest that these are related to the nature of the work rather than to the sex of the worker. Women in skilled and professional jobs do not have conspicuously different attendance rates to men.

It is difficult for unions to reach the women in the catering industry because of this high turnover, large number of small establishments, and substantial proportion of part-timers. John Stevens, the Transport and General Workers Union Official who is in charge of the catering section in London had a membership (May 1975) of 2,500 people. He said it was impossible for him to visit the thousands of tiny establishments where women work. 'I wait for them to contact me now. If they won't stand on their own, no one else can do it for them.'

He indicated the difficulty in working out the legal wages for staff. Three of his most recent members were women who worked as waitresses for a restaurant in a national grill/steak-house chain They had been given the address of the union in an unusual way. To protest against a management decree that they were to change their working hours from twenty-five to thirty-five a week up to sixty hours a week the women determined to hold placards up outside the restaurant telling customers what was happening. They went to their local police station in West London to ask for permission to hold their demonstration and the station officer suggested they join a union, got the number out of the book for them and they rang the Transport and General catering section and arranged to join it on the spot.

The rates the women were earning before tax in 1975 were extremely low. Mary was earning £8 for a thirty-four hour week, Betty was earning £6·25 for a twenty-five hour week, and Stella was earning £8·25 for a thirty-six hour week. This was well below even Wages Councils rates. The Transport and General Workers Union worked out that the women were being cheated of £4/5 a week by the restaurant chain.

There is also a variety of curious schemes in the hotel and catering trade, some of which have the sanction of the Wages Councils and some which do not. There is the – legal–custom of docking up to £3·75 from the statutory minimum wage for a catering worker, by promising that sum in tips. There is the penny for the chef system, which is intended by management to encourage the chef to greater culinary heights. The chef is given, in this system, one penny for every 'cover' (that is, customer) served. This penny comes from the waitresses tips and is deeply resented. Tipping itself is subject to a wild variety of schemes. In some restaurants everyone from the manager to the under chef is expected to receive a proportion of the tips given, in other establishments an automatic surcharge is put on tables over a certain number of covers so that the waitress/waiter is guaranteed a tip, but this does not always happen.

The argument that the catering industry has always used to justify its low wages is that tips make the wages up. But not everyone leaves tips, and waitresses have absolutely no redress if the tips are poor or non-existent. No restaurant manager is going to berate a customer on his staff's behalf. Another alleged advantage of working in catering is that food is provided. Stella described the food in the restaurant in which she worked. 'It was awful. It was all frozen, hamburgers, fish fingers, pasties. Never anything fresh, never anything that the customers got. It was all right for the married women who had to go home and cook for families anyway but it was awful for the single women, 'cos that was their meal.'

There is no doubt that in the middle range of restaurants upwards, where there is a license, and both a lunch time and an evening trade, tips can be good. Mary admitted to £27 a week in tips when trade was steady but said that this did not apply in the catering trade's quiet periods over most of the winter and part of the summer. In unlicensed restaurants – which employ a higher proportion of women than licensed restaurants – tips are much smaller.

The work suited the three women because of their family commitments. But they also said that catering became a way of life, once you had done it you could not go back to anything else. 'You're on the go the whole time, you're never bored,' said Stella. Betty was more pragmatic. 'You're making money all the time, so you don't get bored. The faster you are, the more pleasant you are, the more money you get.'

The Carlton Towers in London is one of the very few unionized hotels. Mrs Mary Keenan is a chambermaid. She cleans thirteen rooms a day and has been a chambermaid for twenty years. 'I like meeting the people even though I don't speak to them. I once worked in a factory and I was bored to tears. The catering trade, although it is the hardest, draws you to it. Once you're in it that's it for good.' She gets, she says, satisfaction from seeing the rooms sparkle, from the companionship of the other women and from the feeling that the management of the hotel is good and fair. The thirty chambermaids are mainly, she says, separated from husbands, divorced or single – their wages are not secondary incomes. They are also middle-aged. 'The management tried to get young girls in not long ago. There were six of them. One didn't last three days and the rest dropped off one by one. One left because she wanted to go to the football on Saturdays and didn't want to work at weekends like we have to. They didn't like hard work.'

But this kind of pride in the work can be abused. One waitress in a steakhouse told an odd tale about uniforms.

'The management introduced these long skirts for us. The restaurant was built on different levels so they weren't practical. We tripped all over the place, we hated them. The customers hated them and the only person who liked them was the director who had designed them. We ripped them so as to stop wearing them – they were very badly made any-way. They were impractical as well, with long narrow skirts and full sleeves which got filthy; and there were no changes of costume. It was hopeless. We felt like Nell Gwynn.'

Such Luddism was the only way in which the women felt they could protest to their employers over these absurd uniforms.

Depressed wage rates in the trade actually create problems for employers, namely staff shortages and high turnover rates. To combat this, parts of the industry rely on casual labour, hired by the day. For employers this is the easy way out. They do not pay insurance stamps or holiday pay; they are not restrained by union labour; payment is by the hour so as soon as the job is finished the casual can be paid off.

The available jobs are predictably the most menial: washing up, kitchen hand, counter hand, waitress. Casual labourers, excluding students and seasonal workers, come mainly from the most deprived and depressed sections of the community. The women are mostly elderly, with a sprinkling of younger ones. They work in this way because they are not suitable for per-manent employment: they are homeless, or they fear the back-log of tax they would be forced to pay if they took on long-term work.

Earnings are comparable to the rest of the industry. For

example, the lowest rates are 50p an hour, rising to about £1 an hour for chefs. However most chefs are men. Most of the jobs available to women fall into the washing-up and kitchen help categories; waitressing jobs are not given to the 'unattractive' or old.

But the short-term advantages of casual work, that is, dodging taxes, do not offset the often shameful treatment that casual workers suffer, or the disagreeable recruitment methods. At the employment exchange specializing in casual labour for the catering trade in Central London, women and men begin queuing early in the morning before the exchange opens. The men, especially, may have to queue all night to ensure a job for the next day. Even then, there is no guarantee that a job will be there for them. If a job is offered them they are fearful of refusing it in case their name is not called again that day. Only the very worst jobs, mostly in the big hotels, are rejected.

'Go as a counter hand, it's a good place to start,' explained one elderly woman, who'd been doing casual work for seven years. 'Once you're put in washing-up you're stuck there. They complained about me to the agency once – I was a counter hand then – and I've never got back there.' One younger woman, tiny, with a pinched face, recounted her washing-up experiences: 'The big places are the worst, they treat you like shit. Yesterday I was cleaning enormous pans for five hours without a break. I didn't get to sit down until 2.30.'

A casual is to be pushed around and is expected to do the jobs no one else wants to do. A casual has no recourse to the normal rights of an employee. She must take what treatment is handed out to her and be grateful if she is offered a job where the other workers are kindly, provide an acceptable meal, and give her time to sit down with a cup of tea for five minutes during a slack period. There is no guarantee, as the casual knows well, that that will be the case.

Many women workers take an unexpected pride in dreary, unregarded mucky jobs. The woman in the Edinburgh bakery whose job was to wash and clean the factory floor and who got down on her hands and knees to extract the dirt from the corners said about her work in the factory, 'We get a good laugh here'.

At the 1969 TUC women's conference one union official suggested that women accept many of the circumstances of dreadful jobs because they believe that to be aggressive would be to be anti-feminine:

> 'Women are told so often that they are patient, conforming, modest, good at routine work and so on that in the end they come to believe it themselves: and a very useful belief it is for employers who want an uncomplaining workforce slaving away unambitiously at routine work on low pay, and for those men – and there are many of them – who are afraid of female competition. One woman trade union official recently remarked that the problems with most women is not to make them work harder but to stop them breaking their backs for a pittance ...' (Muriel Turner, ASTMS)

The pride many women in the service industries take in their jobs can seem like an extension of the pride in keeping a home. But there is no reason why this should be used as an excuse for paying badly.

The pattern of employment in shops has changed drastically over the past twenty years. In multiple groceries and supermarkets the old idea of service, of its skills and importance have been entirely replaced by the importance of displaying goods, encouraging a rapid flow of customers through the store, and replacing goods so that the maximum tempting array is always visible. In all this, the role of the woman shop assistant has been reduced to that of shelf filler (the job description literally encompassing all the duties of the job), check out operator, or cashier.

There are around $1\frac{1}{2}$ million women working in the business of selling. A lot of them work part-time, since the hours and the type of work suits women with families better than many other jobs. In 1975 over 50 per cent of the women employed in retailing were working part-time. This percentage had risen sharply since 1957 when the figure was 31 per cent. The growth in supermarkets was probably one reason for this increase since supermarkets employ large numbers of their shelf fillers and check out operators part-time.

It is probable, too, that the low level of shop-workers' pay has been encouraged by the growth of part-time work, militating as it does against both the organization of workers, as well as against promotion and training.

In a report which came out in 1974 Olive Robinson and John Wallace of Bath University found that sales assistants' wages had fallen relative to those of most other low paid workers. The authors thought that one effect of the *Equal Pay Act*, which came into force at the end of 1975, would be the greater employment of women in retailing – but at a minimum rate which men would not accept. To some extent this has already happened. Diana Jeuda, the research officer for USDAW (Union of Shop, Distributive and Allied Workers) said that the union had, reluctantly, equalized rates of pay in the multiple groceries in 1970 because the men assistants were 'vanishing before our very eyes'. On the other hand, in certain stores like Woolworth's national agreements were made in 1975 to take shop assistants up to the £30 a week level. Despite the fact that this was at a time when the TUC minimum wage level demand stood at £30, the news was greeted by some newspapers and commentators with cries of astonishment at such largesse on the part of the employers.

Women may predominate in distribution, but they are by no means in charge of the shop. Retailing managements have traditionally been reluctant to promote from the counters – where the women work – and a study by the National Economic Development Council (December 1974) found that 60 per cent of the retail organizations interviewed thought that few or none of their shop floor staff had management potential. This view was not shared by the shop floor workers themselves, half of whom wanted promotion and thought they could do a management job. Half the women under twenty-five thought they could do their boss's job just as well as him. USDAW say that the retail trade thinks very little of training and that the fact that the Distribution Training Board was the last of the training boards to be set up (in 1969) is significant.

The pattern of shops and shopping has changed so drastically that its effect on the employee has still not been discussed in much detail. But the changes still going on – with small shops seemingly disappearing weekly all over the country – have meant dramatic changes both in the skills used by employees in shops and supermarkets and in the hours they work.

There is the obvious change in emphasis from selling – often an attractive job for people who knew their customers and were highly regarded by their colleagues. Asking some older women in traditional department stores about their working lives is likely to bring, in return, a kind of testimonial to a type of work now almost extinct. Miss Esme Hale, for instance, worked in the London store, Debenhams, for forty-one years. After forty years she retired, but was asked to come back, to furs, and did 'to help out'. There were aspects of the job which mattered intensely to her – though they did not pay the bills.

'It's not so personal now as it used to be. We used to have 15 fitting rooms, with a bridal room and another for the coronation robes for the peerage. There was a time for everything – Ascot, Henley, the presentations and naturally the garden parties. There were 80 girls in the millinery workrooms and we made all our own flowers. It was, shall I say, fabulous in those days.

I always say you have to analyse each customer, some are quite old buddies, some demand more formality. In furs there's a lot you have to know about each animal, what it eats, where it comes from, what its habits are. Furs are easier to sell than dresses – the ugliest woman can put on a bit of glamorous fur and tell it does something for her immediately. It's difficult sometimes, you have to work out what the customer really likes, not what she thinks she likes. And sometimes a husband may like something more than she does and you don't know whose side to be on. I always say you have to produce a garment that the customer will like within the first three, otherwise its hopeless.'

The passion for work can be stunning. Miss Dellcy Hogbin is in charge of the haberdashery counter of a London store. She gave a hymn of praise to her work.

'Haberdashery is my favourite, small wares, that's what they're termed. You have to have the mind for detailing! That is why I like it. Basically it hasn't changed because it's still cottons and needles and buttons. Harberdashery is so colourful – a customer may come in and thinks she knows what she wants and then there are the colours! And all the silks and threads and zips and binding – and she doesn't know any more! And she really wants help, she wants you to help but often in other places they're told by the girls "Well there are the colours" but they want help. The customers, oh you'd be surprised how happy they leave, especially now they get such rough treatment in other places.

If God blesses you with faculties, then you can keep on while you can. I want to keep on. The busier we are the more I feed on it. You'd be amazed what haberdashery can take – all the buttons and bindings, it all mounts up to a very satisfactory day. That's what you aim for. You see . . . work is my earthly tonic.'

But shop work is not now prestige work. Bright girls are not pushed into it, which is not surprising if the organization of one large London supermarket is typical. Out of seventy-five workers there were thirty-five women working part-time, and every week, the manager said, two or three new girls were employed. But he produced as a long-serving member a woman assistant who had worked at the store for five years. The job requires no training, bar an hour or so for the cashiers. 'Being a cashier is easy – if you are sensible you could learn to do it in an hour. It's only pressing buttons.'

In this supermarket there were five departmental managers and three assistant managers, all of whom were men. The three supervisors (one stage up from assistant) however, were women.

There is discrimination in retailing against women as managers, and no imaginative recruitment of older women who would enjoy and would be good at retail management. It is not well-paid. In 1976 the average gross hourly earnings of full-time women in selling was one of the lowest for women in any occupational group at 87p. But it is work which suits many women, and which could be made better for many women by opening up responsible positions, and by softening the brutal edges of supermarket selling techniques.

The one service industry which does attract girls in their thousands, but is classified as a 'skilled occupation', is hairdressing. Of the miserable 5 per cent of girls who are apprenticed on leaving school, over 80 per cent choose to become hairdressers and manicurists. But unlike other apprenticeships where years of training on a tiny wage lead to substantial financial rewards, hairdressing is not, in general, well-paid. The minimum rates as laid down by the Hairdressing Undertakings Wages Council, in 1975, were £10·50 (in the London area £1 extra) for an apprentice in her first year, rising to £14·50 (London, £15·50) in her last year. Two years' after completing training a hairdresser's statutory minimum wage stood at £24 in 1975.

This is well under the TUC's minimum wage demand of £30 a week, and, according to the New Earnings Survey for 1975, the median gross earnings for full-time female hairdressers (aged eighteen and over, which effectively excludes most apprentices) was £20. This was the lowest of any occupation in the whole New Earnings Survey. Once again, low pay in any industry provides a leading clue to the sex of its workers: in hairdressing almost 90 per cent of hairdressers, out of a total workforce of 96,000, were women (1973).

The popular image of hairdressing – on the fringe of the showbusiness world – is not one that the overwhelming majority of women hairdressers would recognize. Yet, despite poor pay and often uncomfortable conditions, it still has a superficial allure. 'Girls who like looking after hair are like girls who like looking after horses', says Geoffrey Coombs, registrar of the Hairdressing Council. 'They will do it for very little money.' And as with horses, 'success stories' are reserved for the very few. Rose has worked in West End hairdressing for thirty-five years and she has few illusions about her trade. 'There's certainly no glamour in it; the work's too hard and there are too many varicose veins in it for that. A lot of the girls who went into it when it seemed a swinging occupation have left.'

Like many other women who do a job that is underrated and underpaid, Rose's attitude to her work is essentially a caring one. Of her varied and faithful clientele, Rose knows which ones are apt to fall asleep during a hair-do and which ones have to be helped physically to the door and down the stairs.

'I've had the same clients coming to me for years, 15–20 years, and they've followed me from the old salon. Some come up every few weeks from the country. I've been doing one girl's hair ever since she was a child and the other day I had an invitation to her wedding, she was marrying a lord and she begged me to come.'

Rose feels that nowadays young hairdressers don't know how to handle clients – 'It's important to take notice of their wishes or to talk them round tactfully if you really think they want the wrong thing.' She puts this lack of awareness down to bad training, as she does the desultory approach of the girl shampooers. 'It's an art, a gift almost. So many of them are half-hearted, you feel there are great patches of scalp they leave untouched. That's bad training, they must be taught to work back and cover the whole head, get to know the client and whether she likes a hard rub or a gentle one.'

Hairdressing was once a male-dominated craft and it was the post-war boom in hairdressing salons that brought women into it. Now the most fashionable, and the most highly-paid hair-dressers, are men. Rose remembers the days after the war, when the men were in charge. 'They wanted to use you, to get you to do all the donkey work, shampooing, clearing up, handing them the rollers, when you were fully trained.' She has no time for the argument that women like a man to do their hair.

> 'I've often read articles where women are supposed to con-fide all their private lives to their male hairdressers – I think most of that is rubbish. I think many women really prefer a woman to do their hair, they're more relaxed, not so vulner-able, and it's true they do tell you their troubles but on an ordinary day-to-day basis.'

Low wages in farming have driven both men and women away from the land. Yet between 1970–74, when more than 20,000 men left farming, the numbers of full-time women workers actually rose – from 12,990 in June 1970 to 13,300 four years later. As a spokesman from the National Union of Agricultural and Allied Workers said, 'Women are still a cheap and useful source of labour'.

Equal pay came slowly to the farm. By July 1975, six months before the *Equal Pay Act* came into force, women farm workers were paid 87½ per cent of the men's rates. Equal pay had been achieved in the craftmen's grades, but few women qualified for these rates. 'It's not a question of men's and women's work', says Joan Maynard, Labour MP for Sheffield Brightside and ex-Vice President of the Union of Agricultural and Allied Workers. 'It's more the traditional attitude that women get paid less.'

Much of the roughest, if not the heaviest, work used to be done by women and girls, for perhaps half the men's wages. It was a convenient arrangement for the employers: they liked employing women for their dexterity and industry. A. J. Munby, writing in the 1860s about country life talked to some Irish women 'tatergatherers'. They told him: 'We have to be on our

62

knees in the furrows all day long sometimes; scarce ever a chance to straighten one's back.'

Over a hundred years later, Grace Emery, a farm worker from the hop-growing area of Kent, knows that feeling too. 'It's up and down in the hop gardens from one "hill" to the next. You don't have time to stand up before you're bending down again.' Farm work, she says, 'is not easier now, despite mechanization – it's the conditions that have improved. You don't have to be there on the dot. If you've got to take a child to school and you're on piece work you can turn up a bit later. They're not so strict now.'

Mrs Emery works on a farm that employs seven other women workers out of a labour force of twenty. She and her husband, also a labourer on the farm, live in a tied cottage. It's part of the agreement that the wife of the tenant works too. So for Mrs Emery it means full-time work during the summer, with a slack period in the winter months.

There is a clearly maintained line between men and women's work on Mrs Emery's farm. In 1975 the women's rates were 54½p an hour, although in the summer Mrs Emery earned more on piece work. Students are employed on the farm in summer; then the rates are pushed up in the hop gardens since the students would not work for normal rates.

Work on the hops starts at the beginning of May. Training the bines is the women's work. It involves three separate tasks. 'Firsting' is separating the bines out and training them up the strings; 'seconding' involves ripping out the loose bines at the base of the plant; and 'thirding' ('You wear rubber gloves and it's really hot in the summer. My grandmother used to wear finger stools made of rags.') when the surplus leaves have to be stripped off.

Hop picking comes at the end of August. Despite mechanization women are still needed to watch the machines. It is the job that Mrs Emery likes least, and she remembers with some nostalgia the old days.

'We used to take the children into the garden with us. We took our lunch and picked all day. We had a lovely time. Now you're in a shed with two women at one end of the machine watching the hops come through the machine and picking out the leaves and weeds. It's noisy, you have to shout to hear each other. You shift from one foot to another; have a little snooze. By five you're dead. It lasts for about four weeks. Each day seems like a week.'

Strawberry and currant picking is women's work, but apple picking is now men's work. The sorting is done, as it's always been, by women. Mrs Emery recalls the days before cold storage was introduced.

'We knelt in an oast house all day. The apples were kept in straw and you had to burrow into it, make a hole big enough for yourself and one other woman, sort the apples into sizes and then put them into baskets. Now the machines grade the apples, but you have to stand there as they come through putting them into boxes and wrapping them in tissue paper. That's the best bit because you can see an end product.'

Local village women, who used to work in the fields during the summer, now prefer to work in the local factory where there's more money. There are also better wages to be earned on the periphery of farming – in the chicken factories or in mushroom-growing. But Mrs Emery she has no choice except to give her labour to the farm. For Joan Maynard, who was brought up on a farm in Yorkshire, the system of tied cottages bears most heavily on the women. 'The wives used to be forced to work at the farmhouses – it was called "The Hall" – for nothing. It is the women who are most frightened of losing their homes. Women suffer on the humanitarian and economic side from a bad employer.'

The isolated nature of employees in farming means that the individual relationship between farmer and labourer determines wages and conditions to a great extent. Minimum earnings rates are laid down by the Agricultural Wages Council – and anything above this must be negotiated between employer and employee. Traditional assumptions about the place of women workers on the farm die hard. Few women, for instance, drive tractors, although this is a job that requires not strength but acquired skill.

The introduction of machinery to replace human drudges on the farm has not helped women workers. The excuse that women cannot do heavy work, which has barred them from some jobs, has been replaced by the claim that women cannot handle machinery. This has happened in dairying, traditionally a woman's stronghold. The dairymaid used to be regarded as more respectable than her labouring sister, because her work did not bring her into contact with men. Dairymaids were skilled not only in milking but also in skimming milk and butter and cheese-making. The hours were long, sometimes from 4 a.m. to 10 p.m. and, for being protected from the temptations of male company, she was paid less than the women labourers.

Now few women are found in dairying. It has become 'men's work', and where the dairy parlour is large the job will be graded highly. The hours are, of course, still long – beginning early in the morning and running into weekends. Women, perhaps, would not want to sacrifice their lives and families to the demands of a dairying job, but the fact that women have been successfully ousted from the dairy is due to discrimination and not to concern for their welfare.

The numbers of women who work for money in their homes is not known but guesses have been made for two of the most infamous categories – women who mind other people's children and women who do outwork for factories. Working at home is, paradoxically, also one of the ways in which professional women find they can sometimes keep in touch with their firms or professions and firms are often urged to develop the habit to giving research work, computer programming, and one-off projects to women at home in order to prevent both wastage of training and of skill. But this work is for the few, and homework for the poor or unskilled woman can be a trap of gross discomfort. Unsupervised by health or factory inspectors, unknown to any union, unsupported by having other workers around her, the workers at home shows the plight of women at the bottom of the pile.

Child minders have attracted much criticism. But in a country where only one in ten under-fives will go to a nursery, playgroup, or creche, it is hard to see an alternative for thousands of employed mothers.

Figures are hard to come by in this field but one estimate put the number of child minders in the country at 300,000. They are among the worst paid group of full-time workers and it is thought that for many of them earnings average out at about 3p an hour per child (1975 figures). According to Julia McGawley, a research worker with the Child minding Research Unit, the women who do this exhausting and grossly underpaid work fall roughly into four groups. She believes that one type of child minder is the young mother with pre-school children of her own who needs the money and feels she could cope with a few extra children. She may not treat her charges as well as she does her own children.

Then there is the older woman, who may have started out as a child minder during the war when thousands of women were going out to work for the first time. She may be known as a kind of neighbourhood granny and be set in her ways and reluctant to change them. There is also, sadly, a group of women who are childless or in some way obsessed with children. One such woman told Julia McGawley, 'Life without a child is not worth living'. The group which most easily provides good child minders is that formed of women who are genuinely interested in child care itself. But then they set their ambitions higher – they go to work in nursery schools or playgroups since child minding has virtually no status.

In March 1974 there were 30,000 registered child minders and a great many more unregistered minders. The registered minder has had her premises inspected for safety and hygiene and falls within the approval of the law. The unregistered minder may have fearful housing problems. In 1969 a survey of minders in the London Borough of Paddington (by Eva Gregory, Community Relations Commission) revealed disturbing differences between registered and unregistered minders. 71 per cent of the unregistered minders lived in two rooms or less against 18 per cent of the registered. 75 per cent of the unregistered minders were immigrant women whose housing conditions disqualified them from registration though the need for them as minders was obviously crucial.

Local authorities have begun to realize that the child minder – as long as Britain has an abysmal day care system for children – is a vital need for the employed mother. Forty-six London boroughs at the time of writing were taking some action to encourage, train, or assist child minders. Outside London the figure was a pathetic thirteen. The Child Minding Research Unit estimated that around 5,000 minders were being given some such assistance, but this covered only perhaps 1 or 2 per cent of the children in the care of minders.

The National Union of Public Employees has started a drive

to get child minders to register with the union. The research officer, Reg Race, said: 'These women work for economic reasons. When there are more jobs on the market child minders can get better jobs outside so then the supply dries up, but this is the time when mothers who need minders can also find jobs so supply and demand just don't fit.' NUPE wants a wage of £30, paid by the local authority for a forty hour week and training for minders in all aspects of child care. NUPE's view is that minders provide a bank of labour for a future nursery system and that it is essential to realize that the women doing the minding are providing an important service for employed mothers. The Child Minding Research Unit also suggests that child minders should qualify for home helps so that they can concentrate on the children in their care.

At the Angell Daycare Project in the London Borough of Lambeth, a training course has been started by the local authority. It was planned to last for ten weeks taking ten women for two morning sessions a week. After the course the women were to be paid £6·75 per child minded per week by Lambeth Council who recouped a means-tested fee from each parent of a minded child. This was intended to put an end to a situation that is a constant source of worry and conflict for many minders – asking parents for money owed. One minder on the course said that she liked the children she minded, but not their parents. She had problems, she said, with parents who would not pay up at the end of a week. If there was an argument the parents would simply remove the child. Paying minders an adequate wage gives them both a financial security and a sense of the job being worthy of its hire. But training courses give valuable self esteem to child minders. One woman on the Lambeth course said: 'The course is really good because it tells you things you'd never really thought of. I've always just taken having the children for granted, I'd never thought of it as a job.'

In another area of London, Lewisham, the local council organizes a child minding and playgroup section that offers help in the form of a toy library, discussion groups, outings, and talks for its minders. Margaret Driver, who organizes the section, pointed out that one of the problems of the minder – or day-fostering person – is that, unlike a playgroup, she cannot easily raise money for toys or outings. Playgroups can organize coffee mornings, but minders cannot because they are busy minding. Nor are minders usually women used to voluntary activity.

Minders and their clients are often the same kind of women – low paid and without much choice in how they earn a living. A mother may be so beset by financial worries that she is unable to think too deeply about her child's welfare. A minder may be too afraid of being barred from the only job available to her to go for advice or support to a local authority or child care agency.

When all else fails a woman – when she can neither get a place for a child in a suitable nursery nor find a child minder whom she trusts or can pay, or when outside employment is hard to find – can do paid work at home. Some homework is adequately paid and suits women, particularly if they can make a contract directly with the person to whom they are selling their work – home dressmakers sometimes fall into this category. But homeworking, in the main, is not this cosy. 'I would never do it again unless I was really desperate for a couple of pounds', said Celia Whitehouse, the mother of two young children. She was talking about the three months she spent as a homeworker, sewing buttons on to cardboard strips for a local factory at the rate of 61p per thousand buttons. She worked in the evenings, and at an average of three hours work a night she managed to do 3,000 buttons a week. Her earnings for an approximate twenty-one hour week were £1·83.

Celia is one of an estimated quarter-of-a-million homeworkers in the manufacturing industry in Britain. According to a survey of fifty homeworkers carried out by the Low Pay Unit (Brown 1974) the average wage for a forty-five hour week was £5·61. Homework is done almost entirely by women who are forced to work at home because of family responsibilities. For immigrant women, too, homeworking is their only opportunity to earn money because they are reluctant to work outside the home for cultural or language reasons. All homeworkers do it for money – to make ends meet, to buy children clothes and shoes, to have a little extra. As one homeworker wrote: 'Why would any woman undertake slave labour like this for anything but money.'

Sweated labour was the great scourge of the booming industrial age at the end of the nineteenth century – and it was bitterly decried. 'Home labour is sweated labour', wrote Simon Patten in the book *Employment of Women* in 1906. 'It defeats the end of the woman's work and robs it of reward, becoming a dangerous and disintegrating form through which a higher stand of living cannot be attained.' Yet, since then, there have been few attempts to ameliorate the plight of homeworkers.

In 1972 a campaign run by Peggy Edwards, a Nottingham County councillor, drew attention to the appallingly low wages paid to local homeworkers. Nottingham is the centre of the lace industry and there are pockets of the town where lace outwork is a traditional job for women. Ms Edwards found that women were earning between 10p–15p an hour doing dull, routine work in which the only skill is speed.

But Ms Edwards says, in areas of poverty, where even an extra 50p is a lot of money, the homeworkers are frightened of complaining in case they lose their jobs. A Commission on Industrial Relations report (HM Government 1973) mentioned that the same fears led homeworkers to overstate their earning lest adverse comments were made to their employers.

An investigation by a Wages Council into the pay of one Midlands homeworker highlights this predicament. Margaret is a garment-finisher, making loops for belts, and sewing on hooks and eyes. She has two children and 'chose to work at home because neither of them wish to stay at school for their lunch ... My policy is that I am their mother and therefore it is my duty to be there when they want me.' However she disliked asking for money from her husband and wanted to earn some for herself. 'I worked very often for 60 hours a week, weekends included and very rarely do I earn over £10.' Here is an example of some of the prices she was paid: for making two belt loops $\frac{3}{4}''$ long – 1·8p; two belts loops $1\frac{1}{4}''$ long, one press stud, and two buttons – 3·3p. According to her estimation she made on average twenty-six loops per hour which works out at just over 23p per hour. However, the work was not regular and it varied from week to week according to the style of the garments.

When the relevant Wages Council intervened on Margaret's behalf – not on her initiative since she was unaware that she was covered by a Wages Council – it took six months before an agreement with her employers was reached. The factory promised to raise her wages, but since her pay rise the factory has started to machine-braid belt-loops into the dresses, and belt-looping was 90 per cent of her work. Despite the Wages Council investigation, Margaret says, 'My boss says he is not prepared to pay the legal statutory minimum of 58p per hour because of delivery costs to my home'. With an almost complete lack of work, she will have to stop working for this firm. She believes that she will not be given any more work because of the Wages Council's action on her behalf.

This is what homeworkers fear: the loss of work, which in many cases is already irregular. Homeworkers feel vulnerable because they are isolated – they do not know their rights or who to turn to. Trade unions who should, ideally, protect homeworkers in the same way as they do factory workers have found it difficult locating these women, and until recently, have expressed little concern for the welfare and wages of homeworkers. Some union officials would like to see homeworking abolished despite the hardship that would be caused. However, proposals put to the Select Committee of the Employment Protection Bill by the TUC suggest that unions, at last, are putting some weight behind reforming measures.

At present, homeworkers, whether they are crocheting shawls, assembling hair-rollers, making Christmas crackers or fishing tackle, or packing contraceptives are barely protected from employers who spurn the law. The present machinery is neither adequate nor is it effective. The 1961 *Factory Act* requires employers to keep lists of all homeworkers and to submit these to the local council twice a year. The lists have been found to be highly unreliable and the classes of work have not been amended since 1901, and include such categories as the repairing of parasols, leather sorting, and pea picking. One of the TUC's proposals to the Select Committee is that these lists should be made available to unions.

Another of the TUC's proposals is that homeworkers should be paid above the Wages Council's statutory minimum rate to compensate for overheads like lighting and heating. As Harold Gibson, general secretary of the National Union of Hosiery and Knitwear Workers, has said. 'Labour costs account for 25–30 per cent of the wholesale price of the finished article. The rest is met by the employer in providing the working conditions provided by law. When the work is done at home, he opts out of these obligations.' (*Guardian*, January 1975). And because the homeworker is not usually an employee in the normal sense of the word, she does not get sick pay, insurance cover, holiday pay, or a guaranteed flat rate.

It is not only the financial hardship that makes the conditions of homeworkers so disturbing. Many women found working at home disruptive. Margaret the garment-finisher wrote, 'The work is delivered to me in very large bags that take up a great deal of room and there is constant mess of bits of cotton on the carpet while I work'. Other women in the Low Pay Unit's Report complained of fluff and dust in the house, metal filings, or glue ruining the table and carpet in the living room – all these were caused by the work the women did in the home and no allowance was made for them by employers.

The Low Pay Unit's report was highly critical of employers: 'Practically all the firms covered by our survey ruthlessly exploited their homeworkers'. The lack of effective legislation is of course responsible for much of the exploitation of homeworkers, but the fact that most homeworkers are women is in itself telling and provides the most vivid example of how unequal are the rewards of 'women's work'.

FOUR

Professions : only pioneers need apply

Anyone reading newspapers over the past five years would imagine that women, rather in the manner of astronauts, had done the impossible. The news of the first woman judge, the first woman to lead the Opposition, the first woman professor of brewing, the first woman rabbi suggests that there is now very little for women to complain about in employment prospects. If one woman can do it so, the feeling goes, can they all. A useful counter to this list of firsts is trying to spot the tenth woman judge, a female majority in the Cabinet, the female vice-chancellors of British universities. Sightings here will be conspicuous by their absence.

There are few women in management posts, the professions or in the higher grades of jobs in industry. Women in the top ranks of the unions do not match the proportion of women union members, women teachers are not promoted to become heads of schools or departments in proportion to their numbers. A third of top nursing posts are held by men, who make up around 10 per cent of nurses. In trades and industries (food, tobacco, clothing textiles, retailing, and hotel and restaurant management) where women employees outnumber men, women in administrative, managerial, and senior posts can be measured in single figure percentages.

Nor is there anything inevitable about the progress of women towards an equal share of the posts where decisions and policies, which affect male and female employees, are made. In some professional areas, as in skilled, manual work, the proportion of women is actually decreasing.

There have always been a few women who have reached key positions in professional fields, and they have gained enormous respect – often greater than that expressed for their male counterparts – from the public and some of their colleagues. But the gains made by such dedicated professional women in medicine, science, the Civil Service, politics, academic life, and occasionally in business, have not set up a structure in which women are automatically welcomed and accepted in the same way as men. The acceptance gained by professional women in the past has been an acceptance of the exceptional individual rather than the acceptance of women as a professional group.

And this has often been gained after the women made some very harsh personal choices – perhaps giving up thoughts of marriage and children, or deliberately quelling aspects of their personality to fit into a man-made professional structure. Women today are much more concerned to combine a satisfying job with a proper home life than they are to sacrifice one for the other. Furthermore, the changes in the birth rate, marriage age, and women's employment figures, as well as the demands of the economy, all mean that the employed woman can no longer be regarded as an oddity of dubious moral and cultural antecedents.

The statistics given below show the scarcity of women in professional posts. It is the figures for teaching, both in schools and in colleges, and for the Civil Service, which show most clearly the strength of the obstacles in the way of women who want to get to the top, even in those professions where their numbers are already very large.

Women in the Professions.

Architecture   Women formed 4·3 per cent of the membership of the Royal Institute of British Architects in 1974 (1,086 women out of a total of 25,477 members).

Bar Council   Women formed 8 per cent of the membership in 1974 (252 women out of 3,368 members).

Institute of Directors   Women formed 1 per cent of the membership in 1975 (400 women out of 35,000 members).

Medicine   Women doctors formed 27 per cent of the total in 1975 (19,000 out of 86,000). 12 per cent of consultants were women (931 out of 11,164).

Law Society   Women formed 4 per cent of practising solicitors in 1973–4 (1,299 women out of a practising roll of 28,741).

Enginering and allied industries   Women formed 2 per cent of works superintendents and department managers.
   1 per cent of scientists and technicians were women (1972 figures).

Journalism   Women formed 23 per cent of the membership of the National Union of Journalists in 1974 (7,000 women out of 29,500 members).

Teaching   In 1973 there were 10,128 women heads of primary schools in England and Wales and 13,521 male heads. In secondary schools there were 4,295 male heads and 1,050 women heads.

Universities   In 1973–4 11 per cent of teaching and research staff were women. Women formed 1·7 per cent of professors, 6·3 per cent of senior lecturers and readers, 12 per cent of lecturers and assistant lecturers.

By far the largest group of skilled women is the army of secretaries, shorthand writers and typists. The 1971 census listed 737,300 of these, of whom only 1·4 per cent were men. Secretarial work is women's work. It fits the pattern of service that characterizes so much of women's employment. Women are often advised that not only will secretarial work provide secure employment throughout their working life, but that it will also provide a stepping stone into management or executive jobs. This very rarely occurs. Germaine Greer in *The Female Eunuch*, described the secretary as practising a kind of hand-maidenship. In a survey conducted by the Alfred Marks secretarial agency, one of the most determined publicists for all such agencies, it was found that 80 per cent of the 1,000 secretaries interviewed were willing to run errands, 74 per cent were willing to do the shopping for their bosses and for the boss's wife, and 73 per cent felt it was part of their jobs to protect their boss, if possible, from trouble.

One secretary on a national newspaper said that her journalist boss's habit of describing her as 'my colleague' rather than his secretary, girl, or personal assistant, meant a great deal to her. But this small courtesy is not often extended.

Secretarial job advertisements are often exotic. They promise a cast of interesting people and even imply, on occasion, the presence of eligible bachelors. Polly Toynbee described how she followed up an advertisement that read, 'Help! Chaotic office needs Girl Friday [this was before the *Sex Discrimination Act* put an end to such terms] companion, counsellor and co-ordinator for friendly boss in small firm. Exceptional prospects for anyone willing to muck in!' She discovered that the prospective secretary would not actually participate in decisions, not even after some years' experience with the firm, and that her advice would perhaps only be taken in matters of such moment as choosing suitable flowers for the boss's wife (*Cosmopolitan*, December 1974).

Secretarial work can be well paid, enjoyable, can even lead, on rare occasions, to other jobs – the secretary in an advertising agency, for example, can become a copywriter – but these are the exceptions. In the main, once a secretary, always a secretary. Apart from the nature of the job, which is not seen by management as providing a pool of promotable employees, there are difficulties for women themselves in abandoning secretarial work once they are in it. Eleanor Macdonald, a management consultant who is particularly interested in getting women into management jobs, quotes a firm of stockbrokers who wanted to promote five secretaries into the financial side of the firm. But the women refused the offer. They were earning salaries, at the age of 28–30, that were reasonable by secretarial standards and much higher than the salaries they would have had to take for some years while they were training.

Salaries for secretaries, in central London for instance, have been driven up by shortage of labour. But the salary rarely compensates for the tedium of the job. Judy Farquarson, who runs an employment consultancy firm in London pointed out: 'Men often think women can be bought by better money but they don't realise how awful the conditions can be and how badly they treat the women who work for them.'

Women themselves, though, can be reluctant to leave a secretarial job in which, however vicariously, they are privy to important deals and decisions. Mary Mackay, a senior secretary at the Commonwealth Secretariat, said: 'I am in constant touch with what is happening. If I moved over to the administrative side I would lose all that. The decisions might be mine but they would be at a lower level than the ones I know about as a secretary.'

The areas in which it might be natural to look for women in senior jobs are those in which women predominate. Yet, in food retailing, for example, where over two thirds of the employees surveyed in a Department of Employment and Productivity report (quoted in Knight 1974:11) were women in 1968, only 4 per cent of them occupied management jobs. 30 per cent of male employees occupied management posts.

In engineering, where women form 30 per cent of the labour force, they are almost non-existent in management posts. Plessey, which employs a total of 50,000 people, 15,000 of whom are women, had, in 1975, thirty-five women in management grades out of 4,784 people. In one of the largest national insurance companies with a staff of 6,000 of whom a third were women, there were eighteen women above supervisor level, and none above the level of assistant controller. This meant that under 1 per cent of the female employees were in managerial posts compared to 17 per cent of the men.

Ordinary National Diploma	*Salaries after passing*	
Average salary within four years – women	£1,037	(commercial
men	£1,279	catering)
Average salary within four years – women	£1,055	(institutional
men	£1,225	catering)
Higher National Diploma		
Average salary within four years – women	£1,263	(commercial
men	£1,475	catering)
Average salary within four years – women	£1,259	(institutional
men	£1,459	catering)

The arguments traditionally used to explain the lack of

women in senior jobs (no commitment to the job, fear of responsibility, lack of ambition) do not stand close analysis. In the catering industry, for instance, which employs large numbers of women, a report produced by the Hotel and Catering Industry Training Board (HCITB) in 1974 showed that even where men and women started off with the same qualifications, having done the same courses, there was a pattern of discrimination in employment.

Salaries depended on the sex of the worker.

The board says that the women students who come into the industry, in equal numbers with men, are often influenced to take courses in institutional management that lead to hospital, canteen, industrial and schools catering posts, rather than the hotel catering course, which leads to better pay and a greater variety of jobs. Women outnumber men by about four to one in the catering industry but even in welfare catering, where women form 80 per cent of the staff, they only form half the managers and supervisors. In restaurants there are about five men to every two women in supervisory posts, and in hotels the ratio is around two men to one woman. The large hotel groups do not, on the whole, employ women managers. The HCITB says that hotel groups may be quite willing to take women but that women have been 'indoctrinated' against applying. Interviews with women graduates on management courses (quoted in the Board's 1974 report) do not bear this out:

'As a woman I feel that girls should be warned about the limited openings for them in hotel management. Had I been prepared for the prejudice in the industry against women I should have taken a personnel or marketing qualification.'

'I do feel more help in finding suitable positions on leaving college would be an advantage. I did not realise the anti-female attitude.'

'Too much of a man's world. No evident career progression for women. Discrimination against women in the industry.'

There are a number of fields in which women, albeit in fairly small numbers, have been accepted as professionals or managers for a long time. But even here, there is nothing inevitable about progress towards equality. The case of personnel management (in which the majority of women classed as managers are employed) is a good example.

The Institute of Personnel Management has 19,000 members of whom 4,000 are women. The Institute has always had an important female membership but it reported that the proportion of women members, which was 25 per cent in 1965, had dropped to 19 per cent by 1970. The Institute believes this is because the job of a personnel officer is moving 'from elastoplast towards industrial relations'. Women were traditionally thought of as being 'good at welfare' but bad at negotiating and labour relations. 'The increasing realisation of the meaning of personnel management being an integral part of management emphasized the managerial aspect which society accepted as a male function' (Mary Niven, *Personnel Management* 1913–63, quoted by the IPM in evidence to the House of Lords Select Committee on the Anti Discrimination (No 2) Bill).

Social work, one of the 'caring' professions, is another field where equality is thought to exist. Statistics do not bear this out. In 1921 some 60 per cent of social welfare and related workers were women. Forty years on this percentage had dropped to just over 50 per cent. In one field, children's work, the number of women appointed as children's officers dropped from nearly 50 per cent in 1950 to around 30 per cent in 1970 (Walton 1975).

In social services, post-war expansion meant that men were recruited in large numbers for the first time. To attract them, higher salaries and a career structure were introduced and this process generated a professionalism sometimes considered to be peculiarly male.

'In almoning, psychiatric social work and child care women formed a spearhead for professional development and it is a great irony that in a profession so largely fought for over many lifetimes by women that there should be the prospect of long term subjection to men and the fact that principles carefully nursed may be in danger of disintegrating from mechanical and managerial and planning systems.'

(Walton 1975:263)

When a profession which has traditionally relied on the low-paid work of women begins to be better paid it then attracts men. The National Union of Teachers considers that the switch over from women holding a majority of primary school headships (in 1961 there were 10,000 male heads to 12,000 female head teachers in primary schools whereas now the numbers have been neatly reversed) can be linked directly to the introduction, in 1961, of equal pay for teachers.

The numbers, and proportion, of women doctors has steadily increased over the past fifty years, but in science as a whole the reverse is true. There are now fewer women, proportionately, qualifying in biology, mathematics, chemistry, and physics than there were in 1925 (Kelly 1975).

The workings of discrimination, or at least, the rules that govern and dictate the position of women in employment take different forms. Women's membership of the film and television union, the Association of Cinematograph and Television Technicians (ACTT) has dropped over the past two decades.

'Twenty years ago women worked in a fairly wide variety of grades. Now they work in almost complete sexual ghettoes. The opportunities for women to work in many areas of the industry where they do not work now – particularly in the skilled grades in the laboratories and post-production grades in the film studios – came during and shortly after the Second World War. As men returned from the forces many women were eased out. They have now been almost entirely replaced by men. The division between men's and women's jobs has become more and more rigid in the last 20 years, so that many young members assume it has always been, and always will be, like this.'   (Benton 1975)

In political life women have never featured as prominently as they should have done in relation to their numbers. Margaret Thatcher may have become, in 1975, the first woman to lead a political party in Britain, but she was a member of a Parliament in which there were fewer women than there had been ten years earlier.

The Scottish National Party, which has expanded dramatically, had two women MPs in Parliament in 1975, a much better proportion than any other party. But the number of women candidates started to drop when the party had some electoral successes in the early 1970s. This decline shows no sign of levelling off.

'It really does seem as if the more successful we become the more fierce the male competition becomes. There was much more scope in the early days for women on the candidates list because men had more of an eye on the main chance and didn't fancy being failed candidates. But the number of women candidates has conspicuously dropped since the SNP stopped being simply a quixotic venture.'

(Stephen Maxwell, SNP research officer)

The attitudes of men, and sometimes of women, to an enlarged presence of women in managerial professional and senior posts often depend on prejudices, beliefs, and myths, which are hard to disentangle.

'In many men there is a deep rooted dislike, perhaps fear, of women in authority over men. At the same time women, anxious to make the best of a world plainly not geared to their needs, seem to accept the status quo, accommodating themselves as comfortably as possible in a world apparently designed by men for men.'   (Seear 1971)

And in case there should be any doubt that fierce prejudice exists against women in the fields where women are employed, a timely report (published in International Women's Year) produced for the Department of Employment by Audrey Hunt, paints a lurid picture of the evidence.

'A majority of those responsible for the engagement of employees start off with the belief that a woman applicant is likely to be inferior to a man in respect of all the qualities considered important' (Hunt 1975:12). Out of 223 firms studied, the people responsible for hiring proclaimed resoundingly their belief in the inferiority of women. Only 1 per cent of those questioned said that from preference they would hire a woman, 68 per cent said they would hire a man, and 21 per cent said either would do. Only 3 per cent would hire a woman engineer, 80 per cent wanted a male engineer. 15 per cent would have hired a woman to join the sales staff, 45 per cent preferred men. Less than half the managers interviewed thought it would be a good thing if more women occupied senior posts. 'When asked whether there are any ... ways in which the performance of one sex is better than that of the other ... the leading answer in respect of women is that they are better at dull repetitive work ...' (Hunt 1975:14).

Advertisements do not always mirror the views of those who read them, but the following advertisement, which appeared in the magazine *Business Systems and Equipment* in 1975, was aimed at a business readership that the copywriters must have assumed would see nothing amiss in the leering copy. The advertisement from which these excerpts were taken was intended to sell copying machines made by Rank Xerox.

'You don't pay your secretary £40 a week to chase round a table. Or do you?

... The controls are very easy to operate. It's quiet and attractive though it's probably not a patch on your secretary...

It'll never replace your secretary but it will mean that if she's still chasing round tables, she'll need a much better ,reason for doing so!

... In the meantime get her to pull out this page, write your name and address on it and send it back ...'

It is really very hard to imagine women being treated as management candidates by the firm that approved that nonsense.

Women need jobs with proper career structures before they can make substantial inroads into the predominantly male world of better paid, responsible work. It is no good expecting the odd individual secretary to shine so bright that she will be whisked ever upwards in her firm and thus blaze a trail for other women. It has been women's fate to produce many striving and successful individuals in male domains, but no pattern of general acceptance for their sex.

It is often hard for women to get into the jobs that, in the past, have been mostly filled by men. 'It's not the directors but the middle management who may discriminate. It's often those men who don't want female rats let loose on the rat race' (Lady Seear, Interview). And it is often the young or the bad manager who is most reluctant to accept women. A stockbroker told Susanne Griffin, when she was researching attitudes to women in the City, that when the question of women entering the Stock Exchange was first put to a vote it was the young men, rather than the older men, who sabotaged women's chances of entry.

'I've noticed that it's the managers who are not very good at their own jobs who don't encourage young women in management, who don't accept them naturally. I think it's because they feel threatened by a new element.'
(Personnel officer in a food manufacturing company)

It is hard to break the chain that stretches from the belief of many employers that women are neither competent to do, nor ambitious for, certain jobs to the belief of many women that their working lives are stunted by prejudice. 'The girls are their own worst enemy. They don't want a career they just want a job' (Recruitment Officer at the National Westminster Bank).

But this same bank promotes the idea, for instance, that a woman's first loyalty is not to her job but to her family. In explaining why – before the *Equal Pay Act* came into force – the bank would not normally consider giving a company mortgage to a married woman employee in the same position as a male colleague (who 'would normally be sympathetically considered'), a bank official said, 'At the present time we see the provision of the matrimonial home as the responsibility of the husband'.

And in that bank's careers kit, handed out to all aspiring applicants for a job in the bank, a brightly coloured picture showing the layout of a typical bank, depicts the manager's office, the manager's assistant's office and the sub manager's office as entirely the reserve of men. Women lord it over the machine room and the secretarial section and have two posts behind the counter. Pamphlets entitled 'Tomorrow's Banker and his Professional Education' tend to divert attention from the fact that women can be bankers too.

Even entry into many jobs is still hard for women because they may not be considered 'suitable' or because of the prediction of difficulties ahead. Thus British Petroleum say that their women geologists (few in number anyway), are mainly based at head office in London rather than on site in somewhere like Papua, and other oil companies have traditionally been reluctant to send women employees abroad. Gentility is still used as an argument against women's presence in some fields. 'You couldn't have a woman on site/on oil rigs/in a construction yard.' But women engineers do not say that embarrassment, weakness, shock have been any part of their relations with men in traditionally masculine areas. And one woman architect put it more brusquely. 'From my building site experience I have learnt that builders have no particular bias against women architects since they regard all architects as women anyway!' (*Architectural Design*, August 1975). The same woman also said that a woman architect only has to know her job to be accepted on site.

Even when women enter courses for jobs that should in theory lead to careers identical to those followed by men, they can be shunted off into traditional female preoccupations.

> 'We have a lot of very good young women on course but our fear is over what happens to them when they finish. We fear that a lot of them end up in clerical recruitment or in training. They are not, we think, being allowed into the field of industrial relations which is the essential thing today.'
> (Institute of Personnel Management)

At British Oxygen, a company with a tiny number of women in management (2·5% in 1975), but which has looked closely at attitudes to women within its own organization, Barbara Shorter, public relations manager who was, at the time of writing, the most senior woman employee, said:

> 'There are no women line managers whose job it is to run a branch in charge of hourly paid and white collar workers. The attitude is that women can't manage industrial relations because of our culture and the unions' view. It would be a risk if women were put in charge.'

The history of an organization's structure is often responsible, more than individual prejudice, for keeping women on the fringe of some careers. British Petroleum explains its structure like this.

> 'Most of the industrial relations work is done by works managers in the plant. It's difficult to imagine women in, say, a refinery situation. Most of our works managers are in their 50s so to be doing that kind of negotiation in the refineries you would have had to be in the business for 30 years.'
> (BP personnel executive)

BP is a large company and admits that one result of its size is that although discrimination may be frowned upon at head office it is hard to know what is going on in the regions and on site. And anyway: 'The company is more likely to go along with broad social changes than initiate them' (BP personnel executive).

Professional women also stress the difficulties they experience in the social side of their job. Eleanor Macdonald knew of one London banker who arranged lunches with clients or colleagues in clubs where, as he was only too well aware, women were not permitted across the threshold.

The myth that clients do not care to be entertained by women executives is sometimes assiduously cultivated. The reality appears to contradict the myth. Pat Smith, an account executive with a London advertising firm said:

> 'I haven't come across clients who expect me to take them to night clubs or fix them up with a girl. They're usually very straightforward family men. What they do though, is to test you, to see if you can stand the pace. If I go abroad and the client keeps me up late over drinks and then arranges an 8.30 morning meeting I suspect it's to see how I cope.'

Marella Calder, a young Australian shipping lawyer who worked in the City for some years, said that in the shipping community in Britain – though not internationally – she was keenly aware of the multitude of social rituals which effectively keep women on the perimeters of her profession.

> 'Men and women have adopted different systems. For instance here daddy puts down son for X school at birth but not daughters, so that they only effectively get into the system, if they fight, at 20 or 21. In this country a lot of girls simply stop at a certain point and look pretty. And I've found too that a lot of men find it difficult to carry on after work conversation because they worry that they might be acting improperly. But that's discrimination too – it stops me from reaching the same level of social intercourse as men in the same field as me.'

Every woman in a job that is considered part of a male tradition has to work out for herself an image that will be both socially acceptable and will avoid misunderstandings with her male colleagues. 'If you're successful you're accused of using funny methods – chatting people up and so on – and if you're not successful they'll say it's because you're a woman. You have a double bind to get over. First your sex, and then your success' (Marella Calder).

The scientific world is almost literally man-made. The story of Rosalind Franklin, the crystallographer, is much to the point and must be familiar to many women scientists. Her contribution to the discovery of the structure of DNA has only belatedly been recognized. Her colleagues Francis Crick, Maurice Wilkins, and James Watson were awarded the Nobel Prize in 1962 for their work on DNA and in Watson's book on the discovery, *The Double Helix*, Rosalind Franklin is portrayed as argumentative, aggressive, and difficult. Her refusal to play a 'feminine' role frustrated her colleagues. Watson wrote that, while attending a meeting where Franklin was giving a paper, 'Momentarily I wondered how she would look if she took off her glasses and did something novel with her hair'.

Later he appreciated her work. 'Her past uncompromising statements on this matter thus reflected first rate science and not the outpourings of a misguided feminist.' After Franklin's death, Watson wrote in an epilogue to *The Double Helix*, that he had realized 'years too late the struggles that the intelligent woman faces to be accepted by a scientific world which often regards women as mere diversions from serious thinking'.

But the real hazards lying in wait for the woman ascending a company hierarchy or competing for senior jobs come both when she wants to combine a family and employment, and when she wants to return to work after bringing up children. The woman 'returner' finds little encouragement to go back to work at the same level as before, even if she only wants to work part-time.

The obstacles may have nothing to do with any conscious or unconscious prejudice and everything to do with the rate of change in a subject, if it is in a technical field. Dr Elizabeth Laverick, deputy secretary of the Institution of Electrical Engineers, says that it would be almost impossible for a woman to re-enter the electrical engineering field after an absence of even five years, unless she had undergone extensive re-training, which is not easily available. Elizabeth Sadler, a structural engineer with Ove Arup Partners, maintains that she could not imagine balancing a baby on one knee and a set of plans on the other.

Family life appears to dominate much of the thinking of some organizations, such as the major banks when the promotion of women is considered. The commitment of women to their jobs is questioned with doubts centred on the 'She won't go/she won't stay' axis. Either the woman will leave as soon as she has a husband, young children, or changing family circumstances. Or she will not either move home or accept promotion because of her belief that the family must come first.

> 'We've always believed that to be a bank manager you need a wealth of experience which you won't have if you've spent all your life in Carlisle. We have a mobility clause in every contract but the married women are not obliged to take it up. At the moment women are not prepared to be mobile.'
>
> (NatWest official)

In 1971 the Civil Service produced a report on the employment of women in the service. It was a model of enlightenment. It recognized the facts of marital life for many women when it recommended that unpaid leave of up to three years should be available to any woman whose skills the Service wished to retain but who wished to accompany her husband to a place where she could not continue her own career. It recommended in 1971 that there should be no debarring on the grounds of sex, that provisions for leave should take account of a woman's family responsibilities, that opportunities for part-time work should be expanded, and that modifications in the rules be made in order to allow easier reinstatement of women when their children grew older.

> 'It will be an accepted pattern of a married woman's career that she may resign from the Service to care for her children and re-enter later when her family responsibilities have lessened. There are recognised and accepted social reasons for the break in her service and we consider that previous service should be taken into account in determining her conditions of service on reinstatement.'
>
> (Civil Service Department 1971:30)

Most of the recommendations of the report have been implemented. In December 1974 the Government announced that civil servants who had resigned could henceforth apply for reappointment in the grade reached at the time of resignation. 'This will help the Civil Service attract back able people and make proper use of their skills. It will be of particular help to women wanting to pick up the threads of the careers which they left to devote themselves full time to running homes and caring for families' (Lord Lovell-Davis, Lord in Waiting. Government spokesman in the House of Lords, 19 December, 1974).

The rules against employing married women in established, pensionable posts in the Civil Service were only abolished in 1946. Even as recently as 1970 there were still large areas of work in the non-industrial Civil Service from which women were still excluded, though by 1972 most of these had been opened up. The passing of the *Sex Discrimination Act* brought further access to the remaining posts, except for those where the genuine occupational qualification clause applied (this is mainly in the prison service).

But in spite of the thorough and sympathetic 1971 report, and in spite of the fact that its recommendations have, in the main, been put into effect, the staff grades of the Civil Service show much the same pattern as any other profession. In 1974, in the top posts of the Civil Service (under secretary and above), there were 793 men and twenty-four women. In the administrative section of the Diplomatic Service there were 1,101 men and forty-three women. There were 1,083 male assistant secretaries and fifty-three female assistant secretaries. There were 514 male senior principals and sixteen female senior principals.

This is history working itself out of course, and for trends in the future the recruitment figures for administration trainees need to be studied. For the years 1971–4 these figures show two things. One is that the proportion of women applying for administration trainee posts rose from 33 per cent in 1971 to 38 per cent in 1974. The other is that the proportion of women actually recruited from both inside and outside the Civil Service rose not at all – it remained steady at around 33 per cent (figures supplied by the Civil Service Department). If the 1971 report is to have any real effect on the distribution of women within the Civil Service, recruitment figures for the administration grades – which provide the top civil servants – should in the future show an increasing proportion of women.

Shortage of labour can be a great ally of women who want

to combine professional jobs and their family responsibilities. This is particularly true in nursing. In 1972 the Briggs Report on nursing recognized this and said, 'In view of the increasing numbers of women with young children working as nurses or midwives we point out the need for health authorities to consider the provision of day nurseries as an aid to recruitment and retention' (Briggs Report 1972: Para 614).

The report also suggested that the profession needed more mature entrants and suggested a flexible variety of courses designed to accommodate women with varying domestic commitments. It recommended too that National Health Service authorities should create local facilities whereby ex-nurses and midwives could meet regularly and informally, partly for social purposes and partly to keep in touch with professional developments (para 441). This recommendation, however, has not been followed up.

Staffing problems in nursing have been mainly responsible for the much greater participation in recent years of older women in the profession. Briggs pointed out, for instance, that 27 per cent of pupil nurses were aged thirty or more, and over half of all married nurses and midwives return to work. Nursing has thrown up a variety of schemes to help women combine family and work – but more from necessity than understanding.

One South London hospital of 540 beds has begun a nursing 'bank' with the names of nurses who would be willing to do emergency part-time shifts. But this scheme was thought by the shop steward for General and Municipal Workers Union members among the nursing staff to be badly advertised since it attracted very few names. However, Sister Rosie Bateman believed that nurses find it easy to combine nursing with family life since the variety of shifts they can do is wide.

'It's fairly easy for a married woman returning to slot in at a high position and there's a lot of part time work. The night duties here are run by part-time sisters entirely. Also only one of the six nursing officers in the hospital is unmarried which is an indication that it's a relatively easy combination.'

But if nurses find a return to employment fairly easy to combine with responsibilities at home, the married woman doctor who wants to return to practise will find it much more difficult. A third of all women doctors do not practise at all and a third do not work full-time. Part-time women doctors more readily find openings in community health work, family planning, and general practice than in other branches of medicine, which often appear, to young married women in particular, to be operating against the return of women to their profession.

Dr Nina Essex, spokeswoman for a small group of women doctors in London who were trying in 1975 to draw attention to the problems of young doctors with families, said that one of the main reforms that would help part-time doctors to advance and specialize in the profession would be to make the present accreditation system more flexible. This could be done by lowering the number of days a week which have to be worked (then two and a half) to qualify the doctor for a higher post, and by spreading them over a longer period, so that the number of hours of service would not drop, though the minimum numbers of hours a week would. 'If the system were more flexible then women doctors could more often be employed part time in fields like anaesthetics, radiology, and casualty work where continuous in care treatment of patients is not necessary.'

The number of women doctors working in hospitals increased in the decade from 1964–74 by 78 per cent (DHSS, *Health and Personal Social Services Statistics for England*, 1975) but women doctors are likely to find that although entrance to medicine is now much easier, and although they are freer to enter the branches of medicine they choose, when they come to want either to return to work full time or to work part time, recognition of both their needs and the necessity to make use of their skills, is still very limited.

Working part-time at the Bar, or fitting in work as a barrister with family life should, at first sight, be possible, given the long vacations, and the fact that court hours are generally ten in the morning until four in the afternoon. Barristers are self-employed, although they work in a set of chambers, and this would suggest considerable freedom of movement. But in practice, women barristers still feel compelled to avoid any suggestion that they are less committed, competent, punctilious, and reliable than men. They still, in the eyes of many men, have to prove themselves, and this is not best done by taking weeks off for school holidays or turning down briefs. One of the three women QCs at the Bar said firmly, 'You can't do part-time work at the Bar – there is such pressure of space for chambers that people would become resentful of someone only using her chambers part of the time. The clerks would not care for it either and they are the ones who get in the work for their barristers.' This woman came to the Bar after her children had gone to school and a small number of women have taken this course. But Marguerite Russell, one of the younger barristers, says that the Bar must accommodate itself to the idea of women barristers and that the structure has to be changed to make entry as likely for women as it currently is for men.

The hours of many jobs were often laid down when there was no thought that women would ever need to be considered. In Parliament, where sessions often last long into the night, many male MPs have probably found the hours a strain but it has tended to be the women who have drawn attention to this. Maureen Colquhoun, Labour MP for Northampton North, led a delegation of MPs' wives to the Leader of the House to protest. 'The hours are a nonsense for women and for men. We're often tramping round the lobbies at midnight. The thing is that MPs have the power to change it but frankly I don't expect they will, though a Select Committee on hours has been promised.'

All the circumstances of women's employment – family responsibilities, male hostility, and so on – have put a burden on professional women to be 'standard bearers' for their sex. 'If a firm has one bad experience with one woman – then that's it. They think that all women are dreadful thereafter and no good for them' (official of the Institute of Chartered Accountants); and, 'Women who get on have to be better than the men. There's always going to be someone lurking around the corner saying you can't do the job' (Pat Smith, advertising account executive). The feeling is that women are guilty until proved innocent, whereas men are innocent until they are proved incompetent.

One result of these pressures is that women in many sections of business and the professions are more likely than men to retreat into a specialized corner of an organization. They may do it from choice or because they see no alternative. Men who have this inclination are less likely to be allowed to do so: 'The difference was that pressure is put on the men to move in the interests of their careers while it was very rare for any pressure to be put on a woman to move. If the woman wanted to move out or up the pressure had to come from her' (Fogarty *et al.*

1967:61). Add to this the fact that women tend to be more diffident than men – they seek shelters rather than empires – and the process is consolidated.

So women tend to occupy the by-ways of industry and the professions rather than the mainstream; they dominate in the back-up, service areas rather than the power houses. In industry, women find themselves in market research, personnel, advertising, or training – and it is hardly accidental that the ceiling is considerably lower there, both in terms of pay and status, than in other sections of management. Even in professions where the qualities traditionally associated with the 'feminine' touch have been in demand, as in social work, teaching, and nursing, it is the men not the women who are found in most positions of authority.

For example, in social work. 'It is difficult to disentangle the underrating of women from the underrating of caring' (Brooks 1972). What has happened is that women's insistence on, and enjoyment of, personal contact with clients has held them back from moving into the higher-paid jobs where the emphasis is more on administration than on casework.

Similarly, there are many women teachers who are unwilling to give up their classroom jobs in order to improve the equality statistics by applying for promotion into administration. And the same feeling that personal contact, though unsung, is important was voiced by a nursing sister in a South London casualty ward.

'It doesn't bother me that men are coming in at the top. Women are as good as men I should think at administration, but women are better than men at the bedside and so that's where they should be. I'm trained and qualified to work with patients and that's what I want to do.'

Outside the traditional areas of female employment, the same pattern emerges, although in the case of science it would seem that women are being more or less forcefully shoved into jobs that, given an alternative, they would not wish to venture into. The bulk of women scientists, who at post-graduate level are outnumbered by men in a ratio of eight to one, become teachers. A survey of all women entrants into Edinburgh University science faculty in 1972 found out that only 21 per cent wanted to teach and that 53 per cent categorically did not want to teach. This would suggest that of the 50 per cent of qualified women scientists who do teach, there may be many for whom teaching was by no means a first choice (Kelly 1975).

One of the most glaring examples of how women are under-rated, or even ignored, occurs in the little publicized world of patronage. In the inner confines of the Civil Service, there are lists known as 'The Great and Good'. These contain the names of willing and esteemed citizens who are thought suitable for appointment to public boards that advise, direct, and oversee the nationalized industries, public services, and a host of other areas from red deer to the Design Council. According to Maureen Colquhoun MP, 'when it comes to appointing women to public organizations they are not merely regarded as second-class citizens but in some cases it seems, their very existence has been completely overlooked'. Thus, she points out, the Post Office does not have a single woman on its governing body nor does the Electricity Council, Civil Aviation Authority, or the Sugar Board. In 1975 there were only three women (and twenty-five men) on the Design Council and only one woman (ten men) on the Independent Broadcasting Authority.

The rare appointment of women suggests that, although much is generally made of the importance of the family and the vital nature of women's work in the home, policy makers in Government and the Civil Service, as well as in management in industry, do not feel that women, whatever their background, have any experience of value to contribute to public life.

Faced with such assumptions there has been a tendency for women, or at least for those who are determined to compete with men and to widen their opportunities, to underplay their femaleness. Jacqueline Feldman, a French scientific journalist, wrote: 'For many years, I have worked in that world, attempting as far as possible to "live down" the fact that I was a woman – otherwise I would not have been accepted into it.' This was indeed the ploy of traditional feminists, like the pioneer women civil servants who would have been dismissed if they married, or like the women doctors who refused to take a day off to look after a sick child in case it reminded their colleagues that they were women.

This sort of self-denial is beginning to be challenged by the Women's Movement in two different ways. First, feminists are concerned that women should not be penalized for being women and that the fact that they have babies and care for children should be accommodated by the system. Second, the Women's Movement is giving a new direction to the old belief that women should (and can) only be interested in women's affairs. It is trying to effect this by encouraging women to take up women's issues in the work place and not relegating them, as men have tended to do, to the realms of trivia.

For example, it is unlikely that the Government would have brought out the *Sex Discrimination Act* or that the full implications of James White's Abortion (Amendment) Bill would have had such forceful analysis without the resurgence of feminism.

The abortion issue, for instance, was responsible, according to Maureen Colquhoun MP, for making some of the women MPs feel that they should take up specific women's issues. Helene Hayman, Labour MP for Welwyn and Hatfield, said that she realized that if women MPs did not do this, no one would. Ms Colquhoun says : 'The abortion bill has been tremendously important. It has communicated to women outside that we do have something to offer. And from the inside we have found a new liberation.'

The importance of greater female participation in decision-making has been emphasized by Simone Veil, the French minister of Health, who is not notably sympathetic to the Women's Movement.

'I have found that women and men are so different in their approach and concept and in their way of working that the mere fact of a woman taking part in a meeting can change the solution of problems in an important way. If women take part in all fields of our social and economic life and not just in family questions this will, to my mind, produce important changes. This must be wholly beneficial and need not apply specifically to political life.'

(*Guardian* August 6, 1975)

It is hard to quantify just how different women's 'approach' to work is, or exactly what are the special qualities that women bring to their work. And this is a particularly difficult area since it has been the notion of special 'feminine' attributes that has been partly responsible for putting women firmly into the slots – mostly inferior – thought most appropriate for them. But many women believe that women do bring to their work qualities different from those of men, and that it is time such qualities exerted more influence.

Women's new awareness of themselves and of their potential power is gradually gaining some ground in a cross-section of jobs. The medical profession is not noted for its radical thinking, and its top echelons are still very much a male preserve. For instance, only one in every 130 surgeons is a woman. Dr Jean Lawrie, secretary of the Medical Women's Federation, believes that 'surgery is identified as men's work because people see surgeons as gods who can allay the tensions and anxieties of the operating theatre'. However, where women doctors practise in larger numbers, that is in family planning, community health, and as GPs, there are some signs of change. The new Well Woman Clinic, in London, which used to be known as the Marie Stopes clinic, is introducing services to give sympathetic and expert advice on such long-neglected women's complaints as cystitis. Its director Jan Bumstead (quoted in the *Guardian* March 31, 1976) believes that sex problems, like many other medical problems have been treated by father-figure doctors whose presence made women feel 'neurotic'.

Many women patients prefer to share their problems with women doctors, which goes a long way to explaining the success and importance of the Elizabeth Garrett Anderson Hospital, London. This hospital at the time of writing faced with extinction, is one of the few in the country staffed completely by women for the treatment of women.

Like women doctors, women barristers have tended to be corralled in one area of their profession – namely, family law. This is a branch that has never held high status, but with the introduction of legal aid and easier divorce, work in the Family Division courts has greatly increased. This has broadened the scope, as well as increased the fees, of those practising there. But there is, according to Barbara Calvert QC, a great deal of satisfaction in working in areas of such desperate importance to clients.

Women architects are also beginning to suggest that their experiences as women are valid in a professional context. A special edition of *Architectural Design* (August 1975), which was devoted to women architects, mentioned that 'women have had a more practical and sympathetic approach to housing problems and domestic practice'. Santa Raymond, who has set up a

London scheme in which a number of women architects work from home in an informal association, thought that women could communicate with clients who might otherwise be intimidated by the more conventional architectural offices.

However, feminist attempts at changing well-entrenched attitudes in the business and professional world are only just beginning to take effect, and in some areas have little chance of success. Most advertising is aimed at women, and the advertising profession is built around and promotes a facile picture of the average housewife. Women are depicted as almost educationally subnormal, voraciously materialist and immersed in self-delusion. The profession has no wish to change this. 'Provocative ads just don't get the selling message across', said a woman advertising monitor. And by provocative she means, 'showing men polishing the silver. It is just not in an employee's interest to put an idea like that forward.'

In the whole field of women's employment there is little evidence that serious thought is being given, other than by individual women, to both the needs of women and their contribution to jobs. The passing of legislation of itself does not quickly alter the views of employers, nor of employees, that most fields of employment are literally man made for men. If women are to achieve a more equitable distribution throughout all levels of employment, their work pattern – the years at home and a later return to employment outside the home – needs to be more readily accepted and accommodated. And women themselves need to be less modest in the kind and the level of jobs for which they settle.

FIVE

Training: why bother? They'll only marry

'Women workers hoped that training discriminations would disappear when the 1964 Industrial Training Act became fully effective. Its avowed aim was to ensure an adequate supply of properly trained men and women at all levels of industry and to secure an improvement in the quality and efficiency of industrial training. But the impact of the Act on the training of women has been negligible up to the present time ...'

(TUC 1972)

'When I started as a weaver I was 14, I was put under a tenter, a small grumpy man who had two looms. I had a little loom beside this man and I didn't get away for six months from this. I was absolutely terrified of him, he hardly spoke except to point out faults. But I became a good weaver all the same.'

(Mrs Joyce Steddles, warehouse manageress of a Bolton mill)

Training can be anything from a five-year apprenticeship to a Government-sponsored certificate course, to 'sitting next to Nellie'. But at any point on this spectrum there are less women receiving training than there are men. As soon as they enter their first jobs, young men and women head for the divisions that mark their whole working lives.

Destinations of School leavers 1974

	Boys	Girls
apprenticeship	118·2	15·5
professional	3·5	2·2
clerical	19·2	96·3
employment with planned training over 12 months	26·4	13·5
employment with planned training 8 weeks–12 months	20·5	27·5
other employment	86·9	80·9
total	274·8	237·8

(Figures in thousands, Careers Service statistics)

Women are mainly concentrated in jobs which are commonly held to require little more than the exertion of their traditional domestic skills. They work in a much smaller range of occupations than men do, and it is neither easy nor usual for them to break out of these fields.

'Relatively few women are managers or in the professions that support management. At technician level, women in industry are mainly confined to laboratory work. The woman in a skilled job in the manufacturing and production industries is a rarity; around one quarter of female manual workers are in skilled occupations compared with over one half of males.'   (Training Services Agency 1975 : para 2.32)

Women who do receive training do so in a much smaller number of occupations than men. The New Earnings Survey, of 1974, published by the Department of Employment, showed that the 840,000 men receiving vocational training in that year did so in thirty-five occupations, whereas the 393,000 women getting vocational training were employed in only twenty-two occupations.

The modest aspirations of women themselves are often

quoted as being responsible for their absence from skilled or responsible work. Women, it is argued, want jobs that start to pay immediately on leaving school because they expect to get married and baulk at taking up long apprenticeships. When women workers have family responsibilities they are often reluctant to assume further responsibility at work. Many women choosing a job or career are not keen to place themselves in competition with men. For a variety of reasons they are also likely to have fallen behind in educational qualifications (see chapter on education). But the fact that these reasons exist, which they do, is too often used as a blanket excuse for not providing the money and organization that training may require. The fact that these reasons are quite valid is also both ignored and distorted – a proper reluctance to saddle herself with too much responsibility does not have as its corollary a woman's desire to be dumped in an undemanding job for life.

The concentration of women in low status jobs means a low net return for the economy. A report for the Organization for Economic Cooperation and Development looked at the opportunities for and use made of women returning in middle life to employment, and said that economies, as well as women themselves, were the victims of the limited range of women's work.

> 'The need to make better use of manpower is constantly stressed. Yet the position is tolerated, as in the UK, where about three quarters of all women in employment are in jobs which take less than six months to learn. That can only mean that women in the top third of intelligence are employed in semi-skilled work.'   (Seear 1971 : 129)

This wastefulness was shown in a survey on women's employment published in 1968, in which Audrey Hunt reported that when women who had left employment to bring up a family wanted to return to work and found they could not re-enter the fields in which they had originally been trained, they settled for jobs which did not make use of their qualifications. A fifth of the women in the survey had jobs that did not make use of all their skills.

This waste of skills is further compounded by the fact that as the labour market changes its profile, women's employment can suffer by being downgraded or squeezed out. Women's share of skilled jobs has declined considerably this century, and technological change has not increased the range of jobs for women to the same degree as it has done for men.

Between 1951 and 1961 there was a drop in the number of skilled women manual workers from 15·5 per cent of the total female labour force to 13·9 per cent and a rise in semi-skilled and unskilled women (from 28·7 per cent to 32·7 per cent in the latter case) (Manpower Research Unit 1968). On the other hand, since 1964 there has been an increase in the proportion of young men going into apprenticeships and a reduction in the proportion going into jobs with little or no planned training. This same trend has been hardly noticeable among young women.

The trends for the future also give cause for alarm. The Department of Employment predicted in 1975 that the employment of women graduates would alter considerably over the next decade and that up to 25 per cent of them might have to enter traditionally non-graduate employment. This curious prediction did not hold in such a drastic way for men – between only 5 and 10 per cent of male graduates would have to alter their conventional aspirations – a prophecy that may turn out to have been more interesting for its revelation of the worth attached to women graduates' jobs than for its farsightedness.

There are four stages in their working lives outside the home at which women can be trained: when they leave school, when they finish further education, when they return to employment after bringing up a family, and during employment when they either want to expand their job opportunities or are needed in new fields of employment. The major difference between the training needs of men and women is that men do not break off their careers to bring up families (although not all women do this). However, career patterns among men are also changing and ambitious men who switch jobs in pursuit of more money or better opportunities are praised rather than blamed. This change in attitude towards mobility should, ideally, make it easier for women to change jobs, or have breaks in employment – for whatever reasons.

Training for employment in Britain is provided by a variety of means and institutions. The state offers training and training advice through the Training Services Agency, which was set up in 1972 as a subsidiary of the Manpower Services Commission. The state also encourages training, or at least is presumed to, through the Industrial Training Boards (ITBs), which were set up under the 1964 *Industrial Training Act* and which each cover a separate area of industry: construction, distribution, catering, road transport, and so on.

Local education authorities provide around 85 per cent of adult education and this includes vocational courses and day release. Some employers obviously provide on-the-job training. Schools have a large part to play in the training of girls, more so than they do in the training of boys. A large number of girls acquire secretarial training at school but this may be inadequate and can also restrict them from looking at more promising fields than clerical work. In 1974 around 40 per cent of girl school leavers went into clerical work.

'The fact is also noted that in many colleges, girls taking OND in Business Studies are expected to acquire shorthand and typing skills, reflecting the expectations of the colleges that these young women are unlikely to be offered managerial training and are advised to take secretarial skills; to become personal assistants rather than trainee managers, again reflecting assumptions that they will play a supportive role.'

(ILEA 1975)

The great demand by women for further education is shown in these figures: in 1973 a total of 1,973,000 women, compared to 1,544,000 men used establishments in the further education system. But the women studied in the evenings, on the whole, and evening classes are mainly non vocational – 1,174,000 women studied at evening institutes in 1973 compared with 555,000 men, while 176,000 men did full-time and sandwich courses (127,000 women) and 489,000 men did part-time courses during the day (213,000 women) (DES Statistics, 1973).

The lack of comprehensive statistics and the patchy research done on the training of young people has been criticized strongly – by, among others, the Training Services Agency and the Association of Teachers in Technical Institutions. There is general agreement that women are not receiving anything like their fair share of day release courses. The level of day release for young men and young women has remained fairly static since the *Industrial Training Act* was passed (around 20 per cent of all employers under 18), in spite of the 1973 *Employment Training Act*, and much encouragement of day release from certain ITBs. The Expenditure Committee Report on the Employment of Women, published in 1973, pointed out that since 1969 only 10 per cent of young women in employment received day release compared with 39 per cent of young men : 'the improvement of this unsatisfactory situation demands that the day release of young workers in general or vocational education be made statutory requirement on all employers' (House of Commons 1972/3).

This recommendation has not been taken up by the Government at the time of writing, and nor had another equally sound recommendation, that day release and 'adequate training' be provided for young men and women in clerical work. It is another indication of the limited information yielded up on women's training that the Careers Service statistics on the kind of jobs taken up by school leavers have a section for clerical work, which does not distinguish the amount or the quality of the training received.

The setting up of the Industrial Training Boards under the *Industrial Training Act*, 1964, of which there are now twenty-four, has in the main made little difference to the employers' awareness of the importance of training women, although in the 1973 *Employment and Training Act*, the Manpower Services Commission was instructed that it could make arrangements for encouraging increases in the opportunities available to women for training. However, there was nothing mandatory about the instruction. Furthermore, nothing has been done about the suggestion of the House of Commons Expenditure Committee for 'special grants to firms which train girls and women for jobs outside the traditional range of women's work and to firms which provide training and promotional opportunities for women returning to employment as home leavers'.

The majority of ITBs say that they cannot provide information about the training of women in their industries because, they virtuously claim, they do not discriminate in compiling their statistics. This is something they should be made to do, otherwise some ITBs and their officials will be content to rest on statements like the following :

The board ... plays no part in influencing company policies on the employment of either men or women; our advice in this area is confined to matters of attainment, aptitude, intelligence and so forth. As it happens, most employees in the knitted textile industry are women.'

(Knitting, Lace and Net Industry ITB, 1975)

There is now no training board for hairdressing (it was disbanded not long after being set up) though there is a Hairdressing Training Council. Nor is there a clerical training board. Other statements by the boards indicate an unfortunate acceptance of the existing divisions between what men and women are expected to do.

'We find that women are generally in the majority on courses on sales techniques, buying, sales promotion, and display, and that men tend to predominate in courses on financial management and instructional techniques ... the only limitations to [women's] advancement in distribution are those arising from their own [and perhaps their employers] perception of the sort of work upon which they should be engaged.'   (Distributive Industry Training Board, 1975)

'There is no bar to them [women] joining any course, the only restriction is that many of them have domestic ties. In the main we are talking about training at craft and operative level as many of the women are not career minded and therefore not attracted to career courses.'

(Footwear, Leather and Fur Skin Industry Training Board, 1975)

The one industry which women have looked to for a career is hairdressing. But hairdressing shows up the deficiencies of training in a largely single sex field, where the sex is female. The quality of training is hopelessly uneven.

'You will find that in most hairdressers shops there are many apprentices and very few other workers because it is cheaper for employers to use apprentices as unskilled labour and they will be used mainly for things like washing hair and sweeping floors and they will get very little training indeed.'

(Diana Jeuda, research officer USDAW in evidence to the House of Commons Expenditure Committee, 1972)

The distributive trade is another industry that, relying on female labour, has a bad record in providing training and promoting skills. It employs 17 per cent of all female employees and nearly a third of all girls leaving school. After clerical work, distribution – shops, warehouses, mail order firms – employs more women than any other type of work. Most school leavers going into distribution will become sales assistants – and remain so.

According to the Distributive Industry Training Board (itself one of the last training boards to be set up under the 1964 *Industrial Training Act*) less than 2 per cent of staff at any one time are trainees and the majority of these are school leavers. Most sales assistants, the board believes, are hardly given more than a sketchy outline of the job they are expected to do – a look around the stockroom and an explanation of the idio-syncrasies of the cash register. 'Training falls to the supervisors, and of course it should come up to a uniform standard but this doesn't always happen. People in retail tend to live from day to day so they're not as systematic as they might be' (Mary Tucker, ex-training development manager of a large chain store).

Haphazard on-the-job training, which is what most distribu-tive training is, can, by chance, be perfectly adequate; but it also limits the potential scope of many women, as well, no doubt, as rebounding on the employer in the shape of high turnover and indifference towards the job. 'If only management did what they're paid to do and trained our sales assistants, be-cause everyone wants to succeed in their job, even if they don't want to go any further they want to be good sales assistants' (Mary Tucker).

A survey by the Manpower Services Commission *People and Jobs in Distribution* (Institute of Manpower Studies 1974) pointed out that training in distribution varies a great deal. Formal training occurs, not unexpectedly, more widely in large firms than in small companies. However, the Manpower Ser-vices Commission said that, despite the claims of three-quarters of the employers that they do provide training, less than a quarter of those firms who pay levy to the Distribution Industry Board actually claim a grant from the Board to support their training activity.

Supermarkets and self-service chains have further eroded the belief that training is important. Shelf fillers, managers will argue, can come and go. The same attitude prevails towards part-timers, a large section of the distributive trade's workers. The Union of Shop, Distributive and Allied Trades Workers told the House of Commons Expenditure Committee on the employment of women in 1972 that, despite pressure through the training board, it had not been successful in getting the idea of training in the early years of work for young people accepted by employers.

This indifference on the part of the trade towards its young entrants is further emphasized by the dismal day release figures for distribution, which, for girls, are the lowest for any industry. Only 1·9 per cent of girls received day release in 1973, although, it is true that all industries employing large numbers of women (clothing and footwear, textiles, professional, and miscellaneous services) are also those with a very poor day release record.

It is true that many young workers spurn the thought of anything resembling the school they have just left and that a small shop, for instance, cannot afford to spare any of its staff for a day a week, but the reluctance of the retail trade to invest in training has wasted the capabilities of thousands of women.

It is only the larger stores who have an organized approach to training their staff. The College of Distributive Trades in London organizes a variety of full-time, part-time, and refresher courses for around 4,500 students a year, but the college is aware that most of the young women who attend its courses have either been sent by the larger stores or will be put straight on to a management ladder as soon as they enter employment. 'All the women here are keen – they're keener than men. It's marvellous to be able to say to the men that they could do as well as the women if they tried' (textile lecturer). Susan Mitchell, a 20 year old doing HND in marketing and advertising said : 'My friends who haven't had a training treat work much less seriously than we do here. They change jobs more often and really they're filling in time before they get married. It divides you off from previous friends if you're interested in more than clothes, boy friends and settling.' The college does not see an easy way round the problem of how to reach the women not working in the Lewis group or in Harrods. 'The larger stores are organized better. Also they get good people in for training because school careers advisers will direct youngsters into these firms which promote training. And it's more difficult for smaller firms to organize day release.'

The scarcity of training opportunities in distribution with these few exceptions for potential managers, shows how a complacent industry can somehow service its own needs but at the same time allow thousands of women to slip into and out of its employment without skills, prospects or promotion. In distribution this is most apparent with the older women, many of whom are employed only part-time. Mary Tucker, ex-training and development manager of a large chain store: 'The older women who come in part-time often ask to work behind the scenes, for example, in the restaurant area, so they don't have to come into contact with customers. And of course, they will rarely advance from there.'

Yet women workers over 40 years of age make up nearly half of all women employees (Department of Employment 1974, while the forty to forty-nine year old age group accounts for the largest section (over 20 per cent) of all women workers. Well over a third of married women over thirty-five worked in 1971, an increase of 15 per cent over the 1961 figures. Many of these older women are re-entering the labour market after time at home, while some may be working outside the home for the first time.

It is to these women that the clothing industry turns when it is desperate for labour. Employers are being forced to examine their recruitment strategy, for the thousands of girl school leavers who have traditionally been the mainstay of the clothing factories no longer find life as a sewing machinist an attractive proposition. The alternative is the older woman, who has up to now been curtly dismissed as unsuitable trainee material. 'Until recently it has not been thought possible to train anyone over the age of twenty-five as a flat machinist if she has never before used an industrial sewing machine.' This extraordinary contention comes from the introduction to *In Lieu of School Leavers*, a sympathetic inquiry on behalf of the Clothing and Allied Products ITB (1973) into how the industry should reassess its training techniques to accommodate the now much-needed older woman employee.

The intransigence of clothing employers was reflected in the response to an experimental training scheme initiated by the Recruitment, Education, and Training Department of the Wool Employers' Council when they approached 400 firms and asked them to recruit women over thirty for a 12-week training course in the mending of worsted cloth. Only two showed any interest in the scheme, although similar employers had successfully operated the same training course for school leavers (Belbin 1964:8).

It may be that the employers' apathy towards the recruitment of older women stems from a combination of the most commonly held myths about married women workers: they are 'unreliable', therefore spending money on training them is a waste of time; they are slow and inflexible therefore production does not increase. Yet five clothing manufacturers who employed such 'bad risk' employees in a study undertaken by the Industrial Training Research Unit disproved all these beliefs. Turnover and absenteeism were lower among these part-time working mothers than among the younger, full-time workers and training performance had 'exceeded expectations'. At one of the firms studied, in Lincolnshire, 77·3 per cent of the part-timers had reached piece-work rates after six months compared to only 33·6 per cent of the full-timers (Hagger 1973).

Many of the recruitment and training methods used by these firms had been particularly devised to suit older women. And the Clothing and Allied Products ITB has gone some way to consider exactly how older women should be approached, both on recruitment and in training. For example, it suggests that a recruitment campaign should go out into the streets: 'Hire a stall on the local market where work exhibits can be displayed and chats take place.' Special consideration is given to the sensibilities and pride of the potential machinist: 'Adults are irritated and confused by anything they are expected to do which is not realistic.' For example, 'Dexterity tests such as pinboards and ball dropping tests are not seen by older applicants as having any relevance to the job of a sewing machinist.'

One of the problems that traditional training techniques failed to overcome was that older women are often much more meticulous than teenagers. They attach greater importance to the quality of their work but this is often at the expense of speed. Therefore, among the suggestions that the ITRU have put forward for adult training is that exercises should be so easy that they can be performed quickly from the start. 'By grading the exercises carefully, speed and quality have been found to develop together.'

Yet well-thought out training techniques are not the only key to success. The older sewing machinists found the attitude of the production supervisors much harder to bear than the demands of the production line. 'I know they're used to their new people being youngsters but we've got sons and daughters of our own – they didn't need to treat us like 15 year olds too' (Comment from a successfully trained machinist who left her job within a year in *In Lieu of School Leavers*).

Lack of confidence often means that older women are unsuccessful at getting more than a menial job, or if they do succeed, they are unlikely to stay in their job. When Unilever ran a campaign in 1968 to recruit part-time typists none of the applicants were accepted. The ITRU found in a survey of the applicants that Unilever's recruitment approach was at fault. For example, the application form. 'They asked for interests, sports, etc. A housewife hasn't time for many outside interests. It looked as if I'd have to leave it a blank. Then they asked for previous jobs and rates of pay. Mine all seemed out of date. The pay of 20 years ago looked positively stupid.' The same middle-aged applicant was intimidated at interview stage by the surroundings: 'I was amazed by the size of the building ... I was absolutely overawed by the reception lounge and so many little girls – all beautifully dressed – coming and going everywhere.'

The answer to these sorts of fear is seen by Baroness Seear to lie in vocational training in order to 'give [women] self-confidence and a realistic appreciation of what taking a job means' (Seear 1968 : 18). Yet such a service is almost negligible. Out of more than 15,000 women receiving specialist advice in 1974 from Occupational Guidance Service – run by the Employment Service Agency – only 1,635 were women over forty.

One of the few places in Britain to run a course specifically designed for women who may want to return to work after caring for a young family is Hatfield Polytechnic. There, they can find out exactly what they can train for in the future and make the relevant plans to fit training in with domestic ties. Ruth Michaels, who runs the course feels the biggest obstacle for most of her students is the lack of part-time training. 'Our professional associations are extraordinarily shortsighted. They fully educate the 18 year olds who go off and get married, whereas mature students could still give 25 years of work' (*Guardian* December 2, 1975).

Hillcroft College, Surrey, the only all-woman residential college in the country, functions as an academic springboard for women to catch up with academic studies before training in teaching, social work, librarianship, speech therapy, and so on. The ages of the students generally range from 21–45 although there are a few older ones, but 'after 45, women have to shop around to get into higher education courses', admits the principal Janet Cockerill. 'The main problem at first is for those who haven't done any serious reading. But the astonishing thing is the progress in ability and confidence that comes in leaps and bounds.' One woman of fifty-five on a one-year foundation course said that she left school at fifteen, married, and worked as a secretary when her sons went to secondary school. 'I was in such a panic when I started here; I couldn't concentrate. Now it's a bit easier because I feel I have a little knowledge to hang on to as a framework.' She is however concerned about her job prospects: 'I don't know what sort of job I will be able to get. Who will have me, I feel too ancient.'

Fitting in family and work, especially for the non-residential students, is another area of concern. 'We do our best to be flexible to fit in with women's lives. What we do is to pack the time-table solid in the mornings, but there's no formal teaching after four o'clock and day students can often get away early in the afternoon', says Janet Cockerill.

Yet it is only in those traditional fields of women's training – at places like Hillcroft and, for example, the teacher training courses at the Sidney Webb College, London – that any attempt is being made to fit the needs of married women. In another well-trodden path of female employment, clerical and commercial, an experimental part-time course is run by TOPS (Training Opportunities Scheme). Yet in a study of women who had taken part in the course in 1973–74 only 20 per cent had entered part-time work in their training occupation and 25 per cent had failed to gain employment. The Training Services Agency (1975) report comments that although it considers the availability of part-time training fundamental to the achievement of equality of opportunity for women, the economic situation of the time caused a reduction in vacancies for part-time employment.

TOPS also offers opportunities for refresher training, and several courses arranged in response to demand have been supported in cookery, dental training, hairdressing, and office skills. But the overwhelming use of TOPS for women's training

is, not surprisingly, in clerical and commercial courses –
9,145 women in 1973 and 13,435 in 1974 and they formed 80
per cent of all women doing a TOPS training. At the Sight and
Sound typing and shorthand course, run by TOPS in Edinburgh
the women on the course fall into three groups – the divorced or
widowed, women with grown-up families, and the younger ones
changing career or taking training for the first time. 'It's money
and employment the women want', said the Manager of the
course, Marcia Stewart. 'You find out the reasons for them taking the course right away – you can recognize the signs of the
strain some of them are under – I can spot the ones on valium
straight away. They have a lot of strain in their lives, and then
the course itself is a strain.'

Mamie Thom, at forty, is a married woman who after many
years at home was doing the course to see if she still had 'a
bright brain'. 'I wanted to have a new challenge. You get fed
up with talking about the price of Daz and the price of food. I
decided to come here to give me confidence in getting a job with
all those dolly birds in offices.' Audrey Walter was also doing
the course but for different reasons : she is divorced, with two
school-age children, and was then 'unhooking herself from social
security'. By taking training she knew she was losing free dental
care, free school milk, and shoes for the children, but 'I want to
be independent, I don't want that dreadful fate again'.

TOPS approach to training women is not revolutionary :
although women form well over one third of those in training
under the scheme, only a tiny proportion of women attend the
Government 'skill centres' where training is almost exclusively
in traditionally 'male-orientated' occupations. The Training
Services Agency (1975) report lists the numbers of women training under TOPS in 'some men's occupations' and compares the
1973 figures with those for 1974. For example, the biggest increase is in industrial electronics where forty-three women
trained in 1974 compared to one in 1973. Another increase is in
engineering, at craft level, where there was a magnificent total
of eight women trained in 1974 and two in 1973.

Breaking into so called male occupations at a time of high
unemployment – which existed at the time of writing – is not
considered by the TSA as a practical short term way of extend-
ing training to women. The TSA hoped that its report, *Training
Opportunities for Women*, 1975, would show that the points at

which pressure could most usefully be applied existed in women's current occupations. The idea of a mass campaign to turn women into engineers or crane drivers did not, because of money and expenditure of effort, find much favour with the TSA, although the Engineering Industry Training Board began such a scheme, for girls leaving school, in 1976. This plan, to train 100 girls in engineering, over a two-year period, was estimated to cost £500,000. Employers are given a grant as an incentive, to take on the girl apprentices in their second year for on the job training. The TSA pointed out, somewhat sourly, that the cost of training per girl was therefore £5,000.

From the employers there comes a consistent tale of how difficult it is to attract women and girls into non-traditional occupations. To an extent this merely highlights the importance of tackling the problem of low female expectations at school and in the home (given that most young people go into the kind of jobs that their parents have done) but it is not possible to deny that girls' reluctance to venture far from the acceptable route is real and deep rooted.

This is the experience of an engineering firm which has tried to encourage girl school leavers to go into its technician grades and apprenticeships. Out of 400 technicians at the time of writing (1976) only two were women and there was one female apprentice out of 300 skilled employees with apprenticeship backgrounds.

'We have advertised and even given the matter publicity in the local press and in the schools but find that women just do not apply for apprenticeship. We find that very few school leavers are prepared to look at semi skilled engineering work even though the money is much higher than clerical work and the conditions of work are probably as good or better than our office conditions.'

The *Sex Discrimination Act* 1975 allows for positive discrimination in training, and to comply with the spirit as well as the letter of the law it is necessary for girls to be told forcibly that wage rates matter, that it is better to be trained than not, and that there is nothing God given, and everything man made, about the fact that men on the whole earn more than women. The engineering firm just mentioned did have better results with women who returned to work after bringing up families, so that out of 300 semi skilled workers 100 were women, some of whom were doing work previously done by men. The company ran an 'upgrading scheme' to encourage women in this direction.

However a personnel officer with Philips Electrical, which has twenty factories and 55,000 workers, saw the causes of the absence of women in managerial, skilled, and apprentice grades differently.

'For management you need a technical background so you either have to get yourself through a degree or get accepted by the company for a sandwich course – that's six months on the job and six months training. Most of our students are industry based and I would guess there is prejudice against women here. We have not, over the past five years, had any women on industry based sandwich courses. The whole process is a cumulative one, if women don't get taken on as craft apprentices they don't get a chance to be selected for the degree courses from among the apprentices – it's a perpetuating process. It is true that we can't attract school leavers so the majority of women we have are married women who have come back to work – and for them promotion through apprenticeship is over by about the age of 20.'

The job of the school is seen as ever more crucial, in the business of forcing girls to consider wider job choices; the firms that would accept women in traditionally male jobs repeat this litany of reluctance on the part of women themselves. But girls and women are not going to go where they are not welcome – sensibly enough. In the film and television industry, a report found a large and unsatisfied demand among women for vocational training. But there were very few women to be found on technical training courses – under 8 per cent of women employees compared to over 30 per cent of men in a survey carried out on its members by the Association of Cinematograph, Television and Allied Technicians. One of the reasons for this, according to the ACTT report on its women members, is that the 'few in service courses which are available, such as television engineering at Plymouth Polytechnic, or in printing and developing at Kodak, are for those grades where the level of technical knowledge is such that employees cannot be expected to "pick it up on the job" '. They are the areas where the technology changes, and where a 'general knowledge' of electronics or processing is not enough. And these are the areas, the report says, where women do not work (Benton 1975:5).

In a devastating report produced by the Office of Population Censuses and Surveys, on management attitudes to women workers, Audrey Hunt (1975) detailed an almost unbelievable catalogue of prejudice on the part of managers against women. British management does not quite believe that a woman worker is almost bound to be dirty, dishonest, shiftless, and incapable of more than the most menial task, but it nearly does. When managers were asked if they would choose a man or woman for a job, each having identical qualifications and attributes, the only job for which a majority of the managers would choose a woman was in catering or domestic work. Most of the managers responsible for hiring therefore start off with the assumption that a woman applicant is likely to be inferior to a man in all necessary qualities.

Ms Hunt asked the people in firms who make company policy and those who carry it out what could be done to improve women's opportunities by their firm, the Government, or trade unions. She comments drily that 'an interesting feature of the answers to questions is the high percentage who answer that "nothing can be done" '.

SIX

Family : who cares for the children ?

In any rational society where a third of the female labour force was responsible for dependent children the need for provision of facilities outside the home for the care of children would be taken for granted. But our society is so far from being rational on this subject that it only sees fit to provide adequate help for employed mothers when they are almost literally at the end of their tether. Provision nowhere meets demand, and indeed it is Government policy that demand should not be the criterion for providing places for pre-school children, facilities for older children after school hours and in school holidays, or for general relief of families in times of stress.

When Audrey Hunt, in the Government survey Women's Employment (1968 : 107) did an estimate from her sample of the likely demand for child care facilities her figures were so enormous that they greatly alarmed the then Ministry of

Health. The Department inserted a frosty statement into the survey. 'The Ministry of Health states that, as far as day nurseries are concerned, they have been provided by local health authorities since 1945 primarily to meet the needs of certain children for day care on health and welfare grounds. Their service is not intended to meet a demand from working women generally for subsidised day care facilities. The number of places provided is therefore considerably less than the demand shown in the survey.'

Almost three million working women in Britain are responsible for the care of children under sixteen years of age. Of these, 588,600 women have children under five years of age. They represent one fifth of all mothers with children under five. Figures from the 1971 census show how this figure is broken down:

wives (married couples)	543,600	92 per cent
married lone mothers	20,700	4 per cent
widowed mothers	6,200	1 per cent
divorced mothers	10,300	2 per cent
single mothers	7,800	1 per cent
	588,600	100 per cent

These working mothers, of whom nearly a third work full-time, have an estimated 821,000 children under five. The rate of increase in employment for the mothers of under fives has been faster than for all married women under sixty. The increase is calculated as being 63 per cent between 1961–71, compared with an overall increase for married women of 42 per cent (Tizard, Perry, and Moss 1976).

It is reasonable to assume that financial need rather than the desire for 'pin money' (as the anti-feminist tradition had it) is the main reason why women with young children go out to work. However, there are other explanations. Among these is the desire to escape the confines of an isolated and dreary home life. The increasing employment statistics for mothers of young children could also, ironically, reflect the low status of motherhood.

'The achievement of giving birth is only briefly recognised. Many young mothers soon lose their own identity, and come to be regarded (by themselves as much as by others) merely as an extension of their children by day and their husbands by night. So the pressures on women today is to go back to work in order to *participate* in society and not simply for economic reasons.'   (Nandy and Nandy 1975 : 248)

There is also some evidence that the more highly qualified a woman is, the more likely she is to work during marriage and motherhood. Figures from the 1966 Census show that half of all married women with qualifications above 'A' level were employed, which is well above the proportion of all married women who go out to work. These are also the women who are more likely to choose to return to work outside the home for reasons other than financial ones.

For the estimated 821,000 pre-school age children whose mothers go out to work, there were in 1974, in England, 24,552 places in local authority day nurseries. In maintained nursery schools (run by the Department of Education and Science) there were 15,431 full-time places and 30,401 part-time places. In nursery classes attached to primary schools there were 32,527 full-time places and 61,762 part-time places. The total number of under fives in primary schools (this included rising fives in primary classes) was 301,106 in full-time places and 77,972 in part-time places. Total state provision therefore was 449,462 full- and part-time places for the 4,500,000 children under five. Less than one child in ten has a hope of any state pre-school care.

This situation is no accident. For twenty years after the end of the war in 1945, government policy on the care of the children of working mothers was virtually static. Many nurseries closed down so that there were less children in state nursery schools than there had been in 1947. The same thing happened with day nurseries (run by the Department of Health and Social Security), where their numbers dropped from 903 in 1949 to 444 in 1967 (DHSS, *Health and Social Security Statistics*).

The Government gave several reasons for the cutbacks : teachers – then in short supply – were needed for older children; a dramatic rise in the birthrate had created more demand for pre-school facilities than was financially possible : therefore, childcare had suffered from expenditure cuts in the expendable area of the social services.

But the doubts of governments about the wisdom of women

with young children going out to work ('abandoning their infants') were also responsible for the cutbacks in childcare provision. This belief had been set aside conveniently in war time, when it became a 'good thing' for married women to go out to work. 'The belief that parental responsibility would be weakened with the establishment of more facilities for the education of the young child lost its force in the emergency situation. It was now felt that married women ought to work' (Blackstone 1971 :63).

Governments got away with doing very little about nursery provision in the 1950s, and in 1960 the then Conservative Government issued its famous Circular 8/60 in which the Minister of Education forbade any expansion in the number of places in nursery classes. 'No resources can at present be spared for the expansion of nursery education and in particular no teachers can be spared who might otherwise work with children of compulsory school age.'

However, when expediency called four years later, the Government changed its tone slightly. It now instructed local authorities that if nursery places would encourage women teachers back into the profession they should be made available. In 1965, however, the Labour Government took care to say, in an addendum to the 1964 Circular, that nursery education was primarily designed 'for the benefit of children and is only secondarily of value in helping to promote the return to service of married women teachers' (quoted in Blackstone 1971 :68).

In 1966 the Plowden Report on primary education, which was commissioned by the Government in 1963, was published. It is a fascinating microcosm of the attitudes that eddy around the working mother. The committee, under the chairmanship of Lady Plowden, came out strongly in favour of more nursery education – but on the grounds of the needs of the child. The needs of the mother came nowhere in the committee's priorities. Indeed, the report recommended that 'mothers who cannot satisfy the authorities that they have exceptionally good reasons for working should have low priority for full time nurseries for their children' (p. 128).

At the same time the committee was aware of the increase in numbers of employed mothers and of the likelihood that mothers would continue going out to work. 'Our conclusions are that many mothers will work and that their children will, as a result, need places in nurseries.' Yet, another conclusion, to add to the confusion was that, 'It is no business of the education service to encourage mothers to go out to work.'

The Plowden Report did recommend an expansion of nursery education with the emphasis to be put on part-time places. In 1972 its recommendations that there should be full-time nursery places for 15 per cent of three and four year olds, part-time places for 35 per cent of three year olds, and 75 per cent of four year olds by 1982 were accepted by the Government. This would have meant 700,000 full-time nursery class places by 1982 compared with 300,000 in 1972. A £30 million building programme between 1974–76 was scheduled.

However, by 1975, the National Union of Teachers declared that the nursery programme was 'in ruins'. The falling birth rate had been seized by the Government as an excuse for cutting the projection back to 500,000 places, while local authorities had not taken up government grants for nursery school building. Although there was an increase in nursery places of 13,000 between 1973–4, by 1975 the Department of Education and Science told local authorities that 'it is intended to give priority to meeting the needs of disadvantaged children and ... projects are normally to be of minor works size for nursery class provision' (Circular 8/75). Once again the needs of employed mothers, particularly in a time of economic difficulty, were ignored.

To be fair, the Government (and the members of the Plowden Committee) drew on and reflected the prevailing views of a host of experts on child development. The best known of these, and the man who influenced a generation of mothers, was John Bowlby, the British psychologist. In a number of books written in the decade after the war he stressed that prolonged separation of a child from its mother in the first five years of life could do irreparable damage. Most of his research was done in institutions such as children's homes, and from this he deduced that a lack of individual and consistent care from one person crippled a child's emotional potential for ever. Despite the fact that he modified his views in 1956, and distinguished between partial and total separation, the conclusions Bowlby drew were interpreted to mean that only the constant presence of the mother ensured the development of a loving and adjusted personality in the child. He (and his followers) did more, in fact, to keep mothers at home than any chauvinist husband.

Bowlby's legacy – whether intentional or not – has been to leave mothers with the awe-inspiring task of rearing children entirely by their own efforts, without the help of the outside world, or even of fathers. Success or failure, it seemed, depended on a mother's sacrifice and devotion and on very little else. When these views are allied to the strong belief that taking a baby or young child out of the family even for a few hours a day is tantamount to the state taking over the sacred family duty of socializing a child, then it is not surprising that employed mothers have been disgracefully neglected in Britain.

The weight of public opinion also contrived to lay a burden of guilt on the mother who works outside the home. Real guilt is often experienced by mothers over the poor, sometimes disastrous, care their children get while they are at work, but again fewer mothers would be forced into unsatisfactory arrangements if the state did not opt out of its logical responsibilities.

Recent research has now begun to counter the claims of the 'evil working mother' school of thought. It is suggested that the quality of care – from whatever source – and the general home background are the determining factors in a child's happiness. 'Many accusations laid at the door of the working mother are ill founded. Such effects as have been noted are relatively small' (National Children's Bureau 1973).

But there is also the danger that mothers are forced out of the home into savagely monotonous and exploitative jobs by the feeling that life with a small child in a confined and isolated space is worse. To work towards a position where every employed mother has a nursery place for her child is not good enough, since it still leaves the exclusive mother/child bond intact, when all the signs are that the burden of bringing up a child in a modern town or city has to be worked out in some different way. The prospect of the state merely swapping a nursery place in return for the mother's labour is not an appealing one.

The majority of employed mothers make their own arrangements for looking after their young children. Audrey Hunt (1968), found that fathers and relatives looked after pre-school age children in over half of the sample while the mother was working. Only 6 per cent of children under two were in day nurseries, and only 12 per cent of two to four year olds were in either day nurseries or nursery schools. Child minders, friends, or simply taking the child to work or working at home were other solutions.

In 1973 the national study of childhealth and education in the 1970s being carried out at the University of Bristol found that, out of almost 1,000 children studied in the first regional survey, three out of ten had mothers who were working when their children were three and a half years old, and 44 per cent were looked after by their fathers when their mother was at work.

'This fact alone suggests that a high proportion of mothers who need or wish to go out to work must work during periods when the father is home to look after the children i.e., evenings, weekends and sometimes overnight. This clearly puts strains on the family that may have implications for the development of the young child, particularly of pre-school age.' (University of Bristol 1973: Appendix 11)

Relying on grandmother is a tradition that has died hard, but is nonetheless dying.

'It cannot be assumed that when the present generation of children has grown up their mothers will be as willing to accept responsibility for their grandchildren. A grandmother who has worked for many years herself may not feel inclined in her fifties to give up her own job in order to look after her daughter's (or son's) children.' (Hunt 1968:87)

In 1974 the number of children being looked after by registered child minders in England was 85,185 (DHSS, *Health and Social Security Statistics*, March 1974). The numbers of unregistered minders are simply not known, but approximately 100,000 children are left with unregistered child minders each day (Community Relations Commission 1975:55–6). The drawbacks of the child minding system are that the quality of care varies enormously and an employed mother is totally dependent on the goodwill and good health of the child minder for the care of her child. The fees charged by minders also vary, and a reasonable fee for good care can often not be afforded by a poorly paid mother. The system is a haphazard one, but the lack of alternatives may force a mother to accept quite unsatisfactory care for her child.

Many scandals exist within the child minding system. But at its best it can provide a child with a consistent and affectionate background in a home rather than an institution. For the mother, a child minder means the hours of care can fit in with her work, and many mothers feel happier with individual care. For these reasons, it would seem that in a time of economic strain child minding provides the only feasible alternative to no help at all for working mothers.

But the system also lets the Government and local authorities opt out of their responsibilities. There were signs in 1975 that the Department of Education and Science and the Department of Health and Social Security were keen to do just this. The registration system, which is at present the only responsibility local authorities have to child minders, is totally inadequate. What is now needed is money – to be spent on training child minders, monitoring safety and care standards, and providing toys and support services, like clubs and play-groups. Local authorities are reluctant to spend even the minimal amount this would require, but the need is urgent. It should be a spending priority.

Britain's 586 state day nurseries are run by local authorities to conform with standards laid down by the Department of Health and Social Security. There are twice as many private day nurseries in England (1,175) as state nurseries, providing almost the same number of places. In Scotland there were, in 1974, sixty-nine local authority nurseries with 3,355 places, and in Wales there were ten local authority nurseries giving 220 places. Day nurseries open at about 8 am and stay open until 5 or 6 pm, and therefore suit employed mothers more than nursery schools, which keep to school hours and school holidays. Day nurseries, however, charge parents through means testing – charges can range from 12p a day to 150p a day. Nursery schools and nursery classes are free.

The pressure for places in day nurseries is enormous. In 1974, with 24,000 children in English day nurseries, there was a waiting list of 12,000 – half as many children again. And this list only consisted of so called 'priority' cases. The British day nursery system is intended to be purely a life-saving mechanism for the child or parent in a crisis. Even the often drastic need of the employed mother for somewhere reliable and safe to put her child is not considered a good enough reason for allowing her use of the day nursery system. 'You've got to have a real problem to get your child a place – unmarried, divorced, a battered or handicapped child, a handicapped parent or particularly bad housing conditions. If you can't produce that sort of evidence you haven't a hope.' The deputy matron of a day nursery in the London borough of Hackney who said this, also pointed out that if a mother got married then she was expected to remove her child from the nursery to make way for the product of another crisis-torn home.

Local authorities vary considerably in their commitment to the provision of pre-school care. The London area has over a third of the 507 nurseries in England and the North Western region contains about a quarter of all nursery places. The worst provision is in the Northern region covered by Cumberland, Durham, Northumberland, and Westmorland, and in the South-West where Somerset, Devon, Cornwall, and Gloucestershire only provided (in 1974) 945 nursery places.

One of the reasons for the lack of interest in child care and the fate of the employed mother is that the area slips somewhere between central and local Government. It also lacks political status. Tracey Tilley, the chairwoman of the social services committee of Wandsworth, one of London's most sympathetic local authorities, put it like this.

'Nurseries aren't "sexy" in political terms. In the council, day care is "good", it comes in the same category as "the old folk" but it has no one really rooting for it nationally. It's not fashionable, and innovation and experiment aren't encouraged by council officers. And then there's very little impetus from the mothers to improve the system because they are just very, very grateful for getting a place, if they have one, and they find it hard to become involved in campaigning, if they haven't.'

Similar attacks of gratitude afflict women who are able to place their children in company day nurseries. There were, in 1974, some 2,000 places for children in eighty-one factory nurseries in England. The factory nursery has a long history. For example, Fox Brothers Ltd of Somerset first started a nursery in 1835 for the babies of nursing mothers. The infants slept in wooden cots made in the factory while their mothers were given hot drinks after feeding their children. However, factory nurseries have never been an accepted part of industrial life. This is partly because of cost, and partly because 'employers do not consider themselves social service agencies and "are not in the nursery business" ' (Institute of Personnel Management 1975 : 2). Indeed it is likely that most employers do not know – or care – what domestic responsibilities their staff have. Many unions also feel strongly that facilities like day nurseries are used by companies to keep wages low, and to retain the services of women who might otherwise leave.

The main reason companies give for setting up or running day nurseries is the recruitment and retention of labour. It is the recruitment of labour that is the vital factor.

'It should be made clear from the outset that places at a nursery can only be allotted to women going to work in the departments where recruiting is a problem. This is very important, or otherwise the benefits of the nursery to the company will be diluted.' (*Personnel Management* 1970)

Restricting nursery places to the children of new female recruits or skilled staff in short supply is a common, if not invariable, practice. In addition, a nursery place is seen as a privilege not to be abused. 'We don't encourage mothers to visit the nursery during working hours. It causes disruption. We're providing the facility anyway, so it would be wrong to have mothers just tripping off the line to see their kids whenever they felt like it' (Personnel Officer, United Biscuits, Osterley). There can even be a whiff of blackmail about the function of a company nursery.

'Nursery places are likely to be scarce and if a firm can build up a waiting list, it should not hesitate to withdraw the use of this facility if a woman has a bad absenteeism record. The realisation that the nursery place is scarce and sought after is most likely to make women watch their attendance.' (*Personnel Management* 1970)

The paucity of child-care facilities for the employed mother is such that the debate revolves only around children under five. The fate of school age children with employed mothers is virtually ignored, as is the fact that the employed mother may then actually have to give up work. 'When he goes to school I'll have to take a part-time job because of the school holidays and the time between him getting out of school and me getting home. They expect a mother to be at home. I don't know how I'll manage with a part-time job' (unmarried mother, Hackney).

So the employed mother's worries about the care of her child do not end with the arrival of school age. Audrey Hunt's survey (1968) found that there was a greater demand for facilities for children of school age than for pre-school children. Over a third of the women interviewed did not work during school hours, a further third left their child with a husband, relative, or friend, and a fifth said their child could manage alone. During the holidays, a husband, relative, or friend took care of the child in under half the cases, and in over a quarter of cases the child was thought old enough to care for itself. Four per cent employed a minder during the holidays. The use of playgrounds, playgroups, or facilities provided by the local authorities or schools was not mentioned. In fact, when Audrey Hunt asked if any such facilities existed, over 90 per cent of the sample said either that there were not any in their area or that they did not know of any.

Even the scattering of adventure playground and playgroup schemes that did exist rarely fitted into a working life.

'There's a summer holiday scheme in Hounslow in which several schools are opened for the kids – both parents have to go out to work to qualify – that's run by students and paid by the local authority. It's saved me a lot of money and my daughter's been there two years running. It seems very good but the hours are 10–3 so it doesn't solve my problems. It's only a start and it doesn't go very far to provide what we need.'   (unsupported mother, London)

There must also be a whole range of unsatisfactory compromises used by working mothers. Yudkin and Holme (1963) found that a quarter of five to eleven year olds, whose mothers worked full time, had no one to look after them between the end of school and the return of a parent. Almost half the children of this age group ate breakfast after their mother had departed for work, although two thirds of mothers prepared breakfast before they left for work. What is striking is how few fathers, even when the mother is working full time, helped with breakfast.

'I know of one woman who got her children up at 5.30, gave them breakfast and then left for work. The three kids hung around on their own in the house until it was time for school. Then the ten-year-old took the two-year-old across several busy streets to the baby minder and then got himself to school. It was horrific.'

(Tracey Tilley, chairman of Wandsworth Social Services
Committee)

These children were obviously neglected, but the mother could literally see no alternative.

The state has initiated very few experiments to help the working mother. One London local authority, which has thought of the needs of the mother, is Camden. In 1974 the council set up the Langtry Nursery with the aim of encouraging the greater participation of mothers in the day-to-day nursery care of their children. Camden, in common with every other local authority, gives its nursery places to 'social priority' cases. But at Langtry, some of the mothers, who tend to be unsupported, are given a two-year training as nursery nurses.

'We were determined to get them off the supplementary benefit hook. If single mothers last for the five years before a child goes to school, they emerge with all their confidence gone and their skills gone and they're hooked on supplementary for the rest of their natural.'

(Jessica Brill, Head of Camden's day centres)

The alternative to supplementary benefit for many single mothers is full-time work, and social security officers often exert pressure on them to take this up. 'If you take a child away from a mum all day and at night all she has to do is put it to bed, then it's doing neither of them any good', said Mrs Brill. Langtry policy therefore is to encourage mothers to come and see what's happening, and to take part in the nursery. As Yudkin and Holme point out:

'In this matter of mothers going out to work our general social policy is quite hypocritical, while opinion is on the whole opposed to mothers of dependent children going out to work and while official policy in many negative and some positive ways endorses this attitude, these particular mothers [single mothers] are praised for going out to work ... Our social policy too makes it easier for these mothers to take a full-time job, even if they have young children.'

(Yudkin and Holme 1963:70)

The high cost of nursery provision has always been the excuse reluctant local authorities give for not helping employed mothers. The capital cost of a day nursery place at 1975 prices was estimated at around £3,000, and the annual running cost at around £700. A further disadvantage of large, traditional nurseries was shown in 1975 when several local authorities had splendid, empty buildings which they could afford neither to staff nor to run (Horton 1975).

The large nursery has drawbacks in addition to its cost. 'Some of the nurseries are horrific', said Tracey Tilley of Wandsworth Council. 'There's this sort of dividing line at the door over which mothers hand their children. The staff think they're doing well having a mothers' group meeting once a week, run by the matron. It's just about impossible to get a newsletter out or to get staff from different nurseries to meet each other. And we get a bit hung-up too on nursing qualifications, where people come out a bit obsessed with keeping kids clean and medically checked-over.' Yet, she says, there are enormous problems in getting funds from the Department of Health and Social Security for a nursery programme of small, local nurseries catering for between twelve and twenty children in converted houses.

All child care abroad is not invariably better than that provided in Britain, but a number of countries do have more extensive provisions to which they have devoted more thought and money. The emphasis, in countries like Hungary, is on offering the mother of a pre-school age child a choice – to take a job or to stay at home and take up the child allowance. Far from adopting this system, until recently Britain was the only country in Europe where parents did not even get a family allowance for the first child. Hungary has a generous child allowance policy in which a woman who chooses to stay at home with her child can claim an allowance of around a quarter of an average salary until the child is four. In France working mothers with children under three years of age receive child-care allowances to help with the cost of looking after the child.

The United States, where tax allowances for child-care costs were introduced in 1972, sees its role as helping parents buy child care rather than setting up state provision. Such a policy, of keeping state interference to a minimum, is, however, an exception. In most countries, the Government has moved into the child-care arena as the number of working mothers has increased. In Sweden, for example, a labour shortage in the 1960s jogged the Government into action to make it easier for mothers to work outside the home – and during that decade the number of day nurseries trebled. By 1972 there were three pre-school places in organized public and private care for every eight working mothers with pre-school age children. In France the figure is two places for every eight working mothers with children under three years of age. The French Government announced in 1975 a massive programme for setting up 2,000 nurseries and day nurseries over a five year period.

The shortage of State-run pre-school facilities practically everywhere has meant that working mothers use some sort of private day care. In Eastern Europe this task often falls on grandmothers – and is free – while in Western Europe the trend is towards a more organized and paid system of child minding. It would seem that the hazard of the illegal child minder exists even among the efficient Scandinavians, but their approach to the registered child minder is far more sophisticated and careful than in Britain. For example, in Denmark there are some 7,000 child minders who work a forty-one-hour week for which they are paid about £75 a month for each child (no more than two children per child minder is allowed). A rigorous selection procedure is used to ensure that the child is matched with a suitable minder, and there is a special emphasis on making certain that the mother knows and trusts the minder.

The pattern of expanding pre-school child care will hopefully continue, but side-by-side there is a growing dialogue about the needs and wishes of parents and children. Even in the USSR, the introduction of extended maternity leave means that mothers now have the choice to stay at home with their very young children or to go out to work. Other countries have gone a lot further.

Concern that long hours spent in a day nursery may not be that good for young children prompted the Swedish Government, in its 1968 Commission on child centres, to air the idea that parents with young children should not work such long hours – the average working week of working mothers with pre-school age children is now only twenty-eight hours. The Norwegians, too, have taken up this point: their suggestion is that parents of very young children should be able to work a six-hour day with compensation for loss of earnings through taxation or social security. The emphasis is on both parents sharing the care of children and not just mothers. 'We must get away from the attitude that children are primarily the responsibility of the mother. Children are the responsibility and joy of both parents' (Norwegian Minister of Justice, Mrs Inger Valle, at the Council of Europe Ministerial Conference in Oslo, September 1975. Reported in *The Times*, October 3 1975).

This idea is also beginning to filter through in governmental attitudes to the care of a sick child. In Poland either parent can take time off, on full pay, to care for a sick child. New rights in Sweden, introduced in 1974, allow either parent to take up to ten days' leave a year to look after a sick child. More generous sick-leave, but only for mothers, except in the case of one-parent families, exists in Hungary. There, sixty days a year can be taken off work to care for a sick child under three, while for children aged three to six years of age thirty days' leave can be taken. Italy, West Germany, and East Germany all have some provision that allows mothers time off to look after sick children. Such developments, if somewhat piecemeal, at least show that a few governments are exerting themselves to make life easier for employed mothers.

The problems of after-school and holiday care for school children with working mothers have not received much attention, even in those countries with developed pre-school care facilities. The Eastern European countries probably have the most widespread arrangements. Limited attempts to solve these and general domestic problems have been made in Sweden and West Germany by building what are known as 'service houses'. These provide services like a day nursery, youth centre, launderette, shops, and dining room within blocks of 'neighbourhood' flats and so release employed mothers, especially unsupported women with dependants, from many of their domestic chores and worries.

The particular difficulties of the British family where there is only one parent were revealed in a detailed and sympathetic way in the Finer Report (1974). The report showed that on average the fatherless family lived on half the average income of a two-parent family, and that families with a lone father fared almost as badly. The committee, which produced the report under the chairmanship of the late Sir Morris Finer, a High Court judge, made several important recommendations about the help that should be given to one-parent families. Of these, the most significant was the Guaranteed Maintenance Allowance which would be paid to lone parents, and which would replace maintenance. It would be simple to claim, and large enough to offer a real choice between working and not working. It has been estimated that at 1974 cost levels a GMA of £15 a week to all single parents plus increases for children would cost £450 million a year.

But the committee also recommended measures that would cost less and could hence be considered by a government in a time of economic difficulty. There was an urgent need for substantial expansion of day care for under fives, the committee reported. A rather small proportion of the children of one-parent families was found to attend day nurseries (Finer estimated that it was about 5 per cent of the quarter-of-a-million under fives in one-parent families), but this figure is probably a result both of inadequate provision, as well as the fact that often it is difficult or almost impossible to take a job and care for children even with ample nursery places available. The DHSS told the committee that about 55 per cent of all day nursery places were taken up by the children of one-parent families.

The concentration of children in day nurseries from homes where there is only one parent, or from homes that are deprived because of mental illness, poverty, or some form of crisis in day nurseries is an obvious scandal, another example of loading further handicaps on those who start off with a disadvantage. One way out, which the Finer committee suggested, would be to extend the types of child-care offered.

'The expansion of day care services ought not to be channelled primarily into the development of public day nursery facilities; a variety of services is required which takes account of the needs of both parent and child ... in an atmosphere which is socially and emotionally, as well as educationally, satisfactory and which takes account also of the needs of parents whether working away from home or not.'   (Para 8. 129)

This variety should include day fostering, the report said. The Finer Joint Action Committee, a body of representatives from different family organizations set up to press for the implementation of the report, said (in 1975) that the flexibility of day fostering had probably accounted for its great popularity in Sweden where the Government supported four types of day care facilities between 1960 and 1970.

In Sweden, day nursery places had tripled in the decade, places in part-time play schools doubled, and day fostering increased sevenfold. The Joint Action Committee also pointed out that day fostering would meet the needs of mothers with children at school, as well as those of the children received into care (16,000 between March 1972 and March 1973) because of the illness of a parent.

A good vivid summary of what the care of children within a one-parent family can mean in terms of stress and makeshift and worrying arrangements is given by the Leeds branch of Gingerbread, an organization for lone parents:

'The simple fact is that there are not enough nursery schools available in the whole of this city. There are a number of Corporation nurseries who take children on a "points" system and one parent families come near to the top of the list but for those people not living near a Corporation nursery private nurseries have to be used. Charges for these are now running at £6·00 a week per child. A parent with one child therefore has to find a job which pays at least £25 a week just to cover basic living costs, without allowing for clothes, shoes and all the things a growing child needs. Once the child starts full time school, the parent working full time then has to find somebody to care for the child before and after school hours and pay this person. We also have to take on trust that this person is caring for the child properly. We need more nursery schools to enable parents to work and for there to be some place where children can go when school closes to wait for the parent to return from work.'

SEVEN

Rights : with a little help from legislation

Sex discrimination

'The ruthless pursuit of equality by the women's liberation movement – with which I mainly agree – may sweep away the decadent and complacent elements in the male community who seem quite unable to solve the nation's difficulties, or indeed, to justify their place in positions of power and responsibility. One can see this great sweep coming if only because we have not tried women before, after all the centuries of having men in positions of power and responsibility.'

(Lord Houghton of Sowerby. Report Stage of the Sex Discrimination Bill in the House of Lords, July 31, 1975)

There was a great deal of joyous enthusiasm, as well as much apprehension, about the prospect of equality legislation in the years leading up to the passing of the *Sex Discrimination Act* in 1975. The Act, along with the *Equal Pay Act* 1970, came into effect on December 29, 1975 and it covers employment, education bill through Parliament. In the parliamentary session services, and the disposal and management of premises. Women in Northern Ireland had to wait until mid 1976 for the Act to apply to their part of the United Kingdom. Under the Act individuals – including men – can apply to industrial tribunals and civil courts for legal remedies for unlawful discrimination and in certain instances they may be helped by the Equal Opportunities Commission.

The Act, passed by a Labour Government which presented a White Paper on Equality for Women in September 1974, was the culmination of many attempts to get some kind of anti-discrimination legislation on the statute books. Mrs Joyce Butler MP tried four times between 1968–71 to get an anti-discrimination Bill through Parliament. In the parliamentary session 1971–2, Willie Hamilton MP introduced an anti-discrimination bill as a private member's bill but this was talked out on February 28, 1972 by a Conservative MP, Mr Ronald Bell. But a month later Lady Seear succeeded in getting a second reading for an anti-discrimination bill in the House of Lords. This was followed by the setting up of a House of Lords select committee which examined the position of women. The committee published a mass of evidence showing that women were discriminated against in almost every area of their working, educational, and daily lives. In 1973 the Government pledged itself to introduce anti-discrimination legislation in the next session and the present *Sex Discrimination Act* was the result.

In employment the Act makes both direct and indirect discrimination on the grounds of sex or married status illegal. It also makes illegal victimization of anyone who has been involved in any action under the Act or under the *Equal Pay Act*.

Direct sex discrimination has been defined as arising

'where a person treats a woman, on the grounds of her sex, less favourably than he treats, or would treat, a man ... It is not necessary to show that a person openly expressed an intention to treat someone less favourably on the grounds of sex; it will be possible in many instances to infer a discri-

minatory motive from all the circumstances in which the
treatment was given.' (Home Office 1975)

Indirect discrimination is defined in the same (Home Office)
guide as the seeking of conditions from a woman applicant for
a job – like saying that all applicants for a clerk's job must be
six feet tall – that cannot be shown to be justified, that apply
to many fewer women than men, and that are to the detriment
of the woman in question because she cannot comply with the
conditions. Accidental indirect discrimination is illegal too.

The sections of the Act making illegal discrimination on the
grounds of marital status only apply in employment and only
protect married people. The Act does not apply to pay arrangements in employment, which are covered by the *Equal Pay Act*.

The Act is designed to cover discrimination in training,
promotion, and recruitment (one of the most obvious and immediate effects of the Act was the disappearance within days of
'super girl Friday wanted' advertisements and other 'women's'
appointments) but there are exceptions where the Act does not
apply. These are employment in a private household, employment in organizations of less than five people; employment in
religious organizations where a sex bar exists to avoid 'offend-
ing the religious susceptibilities of a significant number of followers'. Exceptions may also be made where a job is held to
require one sex or the other as a 'genuine occupational qualification'. Jobs where a GOQ is held to be necessary include some
acting and modelling jobs, lavatory attendants' jobs, some jobs
in single sex institutions like prisons, jobs where the nature or
location of the establishment means that the person must sleep
in premises which do not have separate arrangements for men
and women.

The Act is not a simple one and the first signs after its passing
were that women and unions were much more enthusiastic
about rooting out discrimination under the *Equal Pay Act* –
judging from the number of cases taken to industrial tribunals
– than they were about using the *Sex Discrimination Act*.

A number of doubts have been voiced. The Women's Liberation Campaign for Legal and Financial Independence pointed
out that lack of nursery facilities in the country meant that
whatever the legislation women were still hamstrung in getting
or retaining better jobs than they were accustomed to. Others

132

pointed out that although discrimination against women in promotion procedures might be relatively easy to prove, cases of discrimination in dismissal or redundancy were more likely to be taken up. 'A woman in a job who is passed over for promotion may wait and hope for a more sympathetic manager, rather than jeopardize her chances with the firm' (Moorehead 1975).

A radical view was taken by the collective which produces Counter Information Services.

'The Act may well be important in terms of women's expectations, but there is little real hope of it changing women's role in society until women themselves consciously organise to do so – and in that situation the existence or otherwise of legislation is going to make little difference.'   (CIS 1976)

However the Act also sets up the Equal Opportunities Commission which has the power to conduct formal investigations in areas covered by the Act when it believes that unlawful discrimination may exist. The EOC's first choice, in September 1976, of an area for such an investigation was the Tameside education authority. The EOC had received complaints that in the allocation of grammar school places girls were being discriminated against. If the EOC, after investigation, is satisfied that discrimination does exist it can issue a non discrimination notice requiring that discrimination cease. If at any time within five years of issuing the notice the EOC finds that discrimination is still going on it can apply to the courts for an injunction to ensure compliance with the law.

The EOC may also assist an individual complainant whose case appears to demonstrate an important principle under the Act. The EOC is solely responsible for taking up alleged discrimination in advertising and cases of pressure or instruction to discriminate unlawfully.

The success of the Act will depend on the willingness of individual women to take their cases to either the industrial tribunals – in employment cases – or the county courts when the case involves the provision of goods, facilities, and services.

It will also depend on the interest of unions in using the Act and advising their members when it may apply. Employers are allowed by the Act to practise 'positive discrimination' to encourage women to take training courses or to join firms where there have hitherto been few women.

The, as yet, unproven ability and will of the Commission both to create a climate of commitment to the ideal of equality and to use its powers of advice and investigation will also be crucial in ensuring that neither the spirit nor the letter of the Act becomes moribund.

Equal pay

Men and women are not paid equally. They are paid unequally: in October 1975 full-time women workers averaged £34·19 a week against £59·58 for full-time men workers – for a variety of reasons which include the historical separation of jobs into 'men's' and 'women's' work, with men's work being given a higher value in both cash and prestige. Women also receive and take up less training and find it difficult to concentrate the same energy on promotion and betterment at work because they take the main responsibility for running the home – in itself a full-time job.

The injustice of women being paid less than men in jobs where their male colleagues receive more basically because they are men has long been apparent. But the history of the struggle for equal pay has been dominated by the two emotions of apathy and fear. The TUC called for equal pay as far back as 1888, and was apathetically in favour of it thereafter. A Royal Commission on equal pay began work in 1944 but by 1946, when it reported, was unable to agree on why women were paid less than men, or on what the effects of equal pay would be.

Women themselves have feared that equal pay would do them out of even the lowly jobs:

There are still women who say "I will lose my job and I would rather work for two pounds less and keep my job". I am getting this from single women who have looked after aged parents and will never marry now. I am getting it from widows and from separated couples and from single girls with babies. They are so afraid because of their commitments that equal pay will cheat them out of something. They are afraid that a man will come along eventually and get their job. Now I have tried to the best of my very humble ability to get it into these people's heads that this is their right, that they will not lose their jobs because any shop steward worth her salt will not allow it to happen. But what I cannot guarantee – is what will happen when the job becomes vacant.'

(General and Municipal Workers Union delegate to TUC conference on equal pay, 1973)

These fears of abuse were not discouraged by many employers and employers' organizations. One industrial relations expert, studying the workings of the 1970 *Equal Pay Act*, said of a number of businesses:

'It's quite fantastic how much they're fiddling – they'll give women equal pay with a low grade of male worker but manage to get men who should be behind the women ahead of them. They succeed in this because of the old shambling pay systems – though systems is too strong a word. In those circumstances it's very easy to change the differentials without anyone knowing.'

The *Equal Pay Act* of 1970 was never meant to bring about equal pay between men and women. There is nothing in the Act to level up the pay of a machinist or kitchen hand (likely to be female) with the pay of a bus driver or sales manager (likely to be male). The Act, by itself, does nothing to spread the area of women's employment from the low paid corrals of the service, textile, and clerical industries to a broader number of occupations where wages are higher.

What the Act was intended to do was to make it illegal for employers to pay different rates to men and women if the work they do is the same, broadly similar, or has been rated as being of equal value. This last category is a vital one – although it is also the cause of disputes over how value is assigned to a job – because it ensures that the millions of women who do not work alongside men come within the Act's remit.

From the passing of the *Equal Pay Act* on 29 May, 1970 employers were given five and a half years to comply with the demands of the new legislation. During this time the Department of Employment monitored the progress of industries towards equal pay. The time allowed was not, it seemed, quite enough for many firms.

'After nearly five years had elapsed there were still nearly a third of agreements and wages orders ... which had women's rates which were less than the men's rates. Furthermore 16 per cent of the employers with manual workers likely to be affected by the Act and 12 per cent of those with non manual workers likely to be similarly affected had made no move towards implementing provisions. Finally there is evidence that many employers who believe that they have either introduced equal pay or have phased plans for introducing it may not have grasped the full implications of the Act for their companies.'

(Department of Employment *Gazette*, August 1975)

The Department also found that, in March 1975, nine months before the Act became effective, employers were often not aware even of the 'broadly similar' requirements of Section I (4) of the Act. The subtleties of the Act in relation to sick pay schemes, preferential mortgages, permanent health schemes (all covered by the Act where they form part of a contract of employment) were also lost on many employers. The *Gazette* report said that in March 1975 industries where women were still being paid less than 84 per cent of the men's rates included hosiery finishing in the Midlands, multiple baking in Scotland, knitwear manufacture in Scotland, and glove manufacture and agriculture in England and Wales.

However it also reported that between 1970 and 1975 the basic hourly rates (excluding overtime and bonus payments) for women rose by 147 per cent for women compared with 113 per cent for men, and it concluded that 'the most likely explanation of these changes is that they are a consequence of the implementation of the *Equal Pay Act*.

It is hard to tell how many women have been affected by the passing of the Act, but because of the peculiar segregation of women's work, it is possible that up to a third – three million women – of the female work force will be unaffected by it. However the Department of Employment estimated in 1975 that some three million women were covered by collective agreements and these agreements, along with employers' pay structures and wages regulation orders made by Wages Councils, bring the women, in theory, within the remit of the Act.

Under the Act, women can win equal pay awards outside any pay policy operating at the time. The Act can also be used to bring men's pay up to a woman's rate, and to give men equality with certain women's allowances. It does not cover pensions, retirement age, maternity or paternity leave, and women are still subject to certain protective legislation.

A woman who believes that she is being denied equal pay can take her case to an industrial tribunal, as can employers and the Secretary of State for Employment. If a tribunal establishes a right to equal treatment the employer has to show that a man is entitled to higher pay and benefits because of a real difference between his work and the woman's – such as length of service, merit, productivity, or a genuine difference in the value of the work done. Where there is a rate of pay for women in a particular category and no men are employed in that category then the female rate must not be less than the lowest male rate in the firm's wages agreement.

In the long term it will be the industrial tribunals that decide what equal pay is. But even before cases reach the tribunals there are a number of ways in which the intention behind the Act – to effect a general improvement in women's rates of pay – can be thwarted. Bonuses and extra payment can discriminate against women but these would be difficult to bring to a tribunal under the Act. Thus firms can give extra payment for unbroken periods of service, for attendance allowances (which penalize those women who have responsibility for sick children, elderly relatives), and for willingness to work overtime. A paper by the trade union research unit at Ruskin College pointed out that real equality of the male/female rate may never be achieved.

'The reason for this is that there are, particularly for white collar workers, many cases where pay depends upon length of service. Thus women who leave employment in their late 20s and return five to ten years later may find that they re-enter on the same scale point as they left. In the meantime their male counterparts have progressed several points up the incremental scale.' (Trade Union Research Unit 1975)

The same paper suggested that unions should do more than merely rely on the Act in the campaign for equal pay by, in general, making their objective 'equal pay for work of equal value' – a wider concept than that implied by the Act – and by ensuring that women are not confined to low paid jobs, by raising the relative position of low paid men, and by ensuring that women are not deprived of the opportunity to work under payment systems other than basic time rates.

In the first six months of the Act, from January to June 1976 569 cases were brought before the industrial tribunals under the *Equal Pay Act* and the *Sex Discrimination Act*. Of these 388 were withdrawn. The success rate, according to the Equal Opportunities Commission, was higher in the second three months than in the first three months (37 per cent against 28 per cent). The vast majority of cases were brought under the *Equal Pay Act*.

Worries were expressed by trade unionists and by organizations monitoring the way tribunals dealt with equal pay claims over the manner in which a number of tribunals differed in their interpretation of the *Equal Pay Act*. Thus an important factor is how tribunals interpret aspects of work, such as a person's experience in a job.

Two cases illustrate how two different tribunals can make different interpretations of the Act. Mrs J. Morland, an order and stock record clerk for Bennett and Fountain Ltd, electrical appliance wholesalers, lost her claim for equal pay with Mr Prigg, the trade counter clerk, although the tribunal agreed that they did the same work in taking orders from customers over the counter and by phone. But Mr Prigg, the tribunal decided, had 'considerable technical knowledge' in dealing with cables abroad, and although Mrs Morland said she had a similar kind of knowledge on the domestic side, the tribunal ruled that 'there is a distinction to be drawn between what can be called real technical knowledge and the knowledge which merely related to the things which are being dealt with'.

But on March 31, sales clerk Mrs J. K. Parsons won parity with sales clerk Mr French in the London office of Gomshall and Associated Tanneries, although the firm claimed that Mr French had more experience in dealing with foreign sales than Mrs Parsons. The tribunal granted the claim, saying that Mrs Parsons would master foreign sales, if given the chance, and anyway had considerable experience in home sales. (Cases quoted by Anna Coote 1976.)

The first claimant under the Act, Mrs Ann Hunt, a wallpaper stock controller, lost her claim to parity with a male colleague in the same grade because the Birmingham tribunal, on March 1, 1976 ruled that the man's extra £481 per annum was genuinely due to material differences related to outside contracts and the greater number of promotions of paints (which the man handled) as opposed to wallcoverings. But, the tribunal also said, that, 'to a lesser extent the respondents were entitled to take into account the past experience of the man and the background to his appointment'.

The extent to which tribunals take into account factors like experience – and most women lack the uninterrupted work experience of most men – will be crucial to the way in which the Act brings about greater parity between the pay of men and women. The difficult job of the tribunals is to interpret exactly what a material difference is, and although much of their work must concentrate on interpreting the loosely phrased requirements in the Act, too much interpretative judgment could discriminate against women applicants.

'The major problem of the tribunals' involvement in equal pay may be that they begin to make decisions based not only on the terms of the Act, but on criteria which the tribunal considers important ... it should not be a tribunal's job to play St George, or the Victorian father and bring into play questions of merit service, or even justice. The tribunals have to apply the Act – and only that.'

(Incomes Data Services Ltd 1976)

The tribunals also do not have the power to examine wage agreements, which may often be discriminatory against women – in giving greater value to men's physical strength for instance, or in grading the jobs done mainly by women at the bottom end of the grading scale.

The Act does not cover curious cases like that of Mrs Susan Waddington, a Leicester social worker, whose claim for equal pay with a junior male colleague was dismissed on the grounds that their jobs were not of equal value – hers being the more responsible and senior (*Guardian* April 29, 1976). Nor does it help women who believe they work harder and are more valuable to their employers than men doing similar work (Case of Mrs M. R. Idiers v the Belle Vue Laundry Group, Shrewsbury Industrial Tribunal March 11, 1976).

The Trico strike – the most spectacular action brought by women workers who believed they had a right to equal pay and went on strike for over four months in their determination to get it – showed the difficulties of interpreting the Act in so called 'red circle' jobs. Five men at a windscreen wiper factory in Middlesex were transferred from the night shift to the day shift – mainly staffed by women – and kept their higher night shift rates. The women demanded parity with the men, the management refused, and an industrial tribunal agreed that the case did not fall within the area of the *Equal Pay Act*. The women's union, the AUEW (the Engineering Union) took the tribunal decision as an affirmation of its belief that the Act is not sufficiently favourable to women workers to make a marked difference in narrowing the gap between male and female wages.

But the Act has probably brought about some narrowing of the gap in rates – which had been widening in the twenty years before the Act was passed in 1970 and it has made some women more aware of their possible legal right to equal pay, and others aware of the gap between male and female rates based on nothing more than, in many cases, a mere difference in sex. The Act may also influence the negotiation of wage agreements between unions and employers well before individual cases have to be taken to tribunals.

Protective legislation

Women have been protected by law from working excessively long hours, doing shift work and night work since the middle of the nineteenth century. Scandalous conditions at work prompted Victorian reformers, following legislation restricting the employment of children and young people, to extend this to women. And in 1847 the *Ten Hours Act*, under heavy fire from manufacturers who regarded the Act as 'repressive', was passed. It reduced the maximum working hours for women and young persons in textile factories to 10 hours per day, or fifty-eight hours per week. Later, the principle of factory regulation was extended to other industries besides textiles. Agitation for such reform was born out of humanitarian ideas, but it was also linked with a middle-class fear that family life would be destroyed if women's employment were allowed to continue unchecked. Lord Shaftesbury, whose *Mines Act* of 1842 forbade women and children under ten years of age to go down mines, said: 'Domestic life and domestic discipline must soon be at an end; society will consist of individuals no longer grouped in families;

so early is the separation of husband and wife.'

The basic provisions governing the employment of women, encompassed in a handful of Acts, state that women in factories cannot work for more than nine hours a day or 48 hours a week, nor can they start work before 7.00 am, or finish after 8.00 pm during the week and 1.00 pm on Saturdays. Women are forbidden to work at all on Sundays. The maximum continuous working spell for women is four and a half hours, which may be increased to five hours if they have a ten-minute break. The laws governing hours of work also include a limit to the amount of overtime women may work: this has been set at a maximum of six hours a week and 100 hours a year.

There are however, exceptions to the rule in many industries. Some are the result of general exemption orders granted as long ago as the 1930s. And since then there has been practically no inquiry into the rights and wrongs of these provisions. For example, women making bread, flour, confectionery, or sausages can work a total of ten hours a day on two days a week other than Saturday. They may start work at 6.00 am (one hour earlier than is otherwise legal) and stop work at 9.00 pm (one hour later than is otherwise legal). The same laws apply to laundry workers. In the dairy industry the hours of work have been further expanded: women can work up to fifty-four hours per week, and in cheese factories, during certain times of year, working hours can be increased to sixty hours per week.

These limits apply to factories, but there are many work places – offices, railway premises, hospitals, and farms – that are not covered by legislation limiting hours. The Acts also do not apply 'to women holding responsible positions of management who are not ordinarily engaged in manual work.'

Over and above those workers outside the legislation are those who are excluded by virtue of special exemption orders. These orders, which are granted yearly by the Secretary of State for Employment, allow women to work hours otherwise deemed illegal. In practice, it means that women are allowed to do shift work, which may include working at nights. The powers of the Minister are such that he can grant a special exemption order if 'it is desirable in the public interest to do so for the purposes of maintaining or increasing the efficiency of industry or transport.'

The machinery for granting special exemption orders is

through the offices of the Health and Safety Executive, which incorporates the Factory Inspectorate. Employers apply to their district inspectors who visit the factory, inquire into welfare and safety conditions, and canvas the workers about their feelings towards the lifting of the Factory Acts limiting hours.

The numbers of applications for special exemption orders are not known, but they are fairly freely granted and once granted they are rarely revoked. A spokesman from the Health and Safety Executive said that it would not use its powers to grant or to refuse special exemption orders in order to discriminate against women in favour of male employment, but that it would take into consideration the immediate local unemployment situation.

Over 213,000 women workers are affected by special exemption orders (July 1975 figures). Over the past decade there has been a gradual increase in the numbers of women involved, and there seems to be no sign that the trend will change. There are various reasons for the increase: the growing numbers of employed women, new factories opening in development areas and the tendency for employers to keep their machinery going twenty-four hours a day.

The largest group of women under special exemption orders are the food, drink, and tobacco workers (nearly 60,000 of them in 1974), closely followed by the electrical and engineering workers.

The existence and increasing use of both general and special exemption orders is seen as one of the main weaknesses in the protective laws by those who want to see them abolished. And over the last ten years pressure has mounted for their repeal.

At present, the Equal Opportunities Commission, with the Health and Safety Executive, has been given the task of looking into the protective laws. Its review is due to be completed by the beginning of 1978.

Much of the debate has centred around the thorny problem of whether 'protective' can be interpreted as 'discriminatory'. The repealers maintain that the existing laws should be swept away since there is now no good reason why women should be restricted from working where and when they like. This was the position taken up by the Institute of Personnel Management in its policy statement *Women and Employment*. It said it saw 'no reason why women should not be allowed to decide for themselves what is good for them and have the same freedom as men to determine with their employers what their hours of work should be'.

This was also very much the view of the Confederation of British Industry in a Department of Employment report in 1969 on the *Hours of Employment of Women and Young Persons Employed in Factories*. The CBI drew attention to the fact that waitresses, bus conductresses, and nurses worked at night, by virtue of the requirements of their jobs. The two sides of industry who drew up the Department of Employment's report failed to agree on the future of the factory laws. Employers were in favour of repeal, while the TUC favoured retention. The TUC are, in fact, against shift and night work for men as well as for women because of its disruptive effect on all workers' lives.

Official TUC policy, however, does not necessarily represent the opinions of the grass roots of the union movement. There is debate between men and women and between women and women as to the merits of protective legislation. Those who are against repeal argue that to do away with the laws will weaken women's position at work. Ms Terry Marsland of the Tobacco Workers' Union says : 'We're opposed to any wholesale repeal. The demand for it arises out of the *Sex Discrimination Act* and it is appalling that this might be the price that women have to pay for equality.' Such a price, however, is exactly what some women unionists want, and they feel that freeing women from protective legislation will, while men are still required to work all hours, give then equality. Hattie Brierlay, shop steward of the General and Municipal Workers' Union, at a sweet factory in the north-east, feels that women should have such a choice. She quotes a case in point :

'The factory wanted to include a night shift on the pastille tube section, as well as a day and evening shift, because demand had gone up. The women wanted the night work, but the men were put in instead. The women should have the right of choice, and with the fear of unemployment I don't want to be protected. Anyhow, the factory wanted the women because they said they could do the job more efficiently.'

Certainly there are women who like night work – mostly the

143

single or the middle-aged. But for the mother with a young family night work is often an added burden. Indeed, the TUC's line, which is not unlike that of the nineteenth-century reformers, points to the effect of night work on family life. 'Neglect of their [women's] responsibilities may have serious social consequences in regard to family life, juvenile delinquency etc' (Department of Employment 1969:7).

The repeal of protective legislation may also be harmful to the woman herself, who is, in effect, on a *permanent* 'double shift', at work and at home.

> 'Although there is no apparent physiological reason why women should not be employed on the night shift as well as men or from the viewpoint of their ability to work, there are some social reasons which might make it inadvisable. First, women who have the responsibility of children or aged persons often cannot arrange their households to fit a night schedule. It may be more difficult to obtain the proper rest during the daytime than at night and, with household duties added to factory work, undisturbed sleep is essential.'
>
> (Baetjer 1948:26)

This is what a domestic supervisor at a West London hospital had to say about night work.

> 'The strain was hardest on nights. I'm quite strong and my body adjusted. But some of the girls had kids running about all day while they were trying to sleep. Their attendance was very bad. I don't think a week went by without 10 or 12 of them being off sick.'
>
> (National Council of Civil Liberties 1975)

The detrimental effect on health from shift work is still largely a matter of guesswork. Evidence is patchy largely because there has been so little research into occupational health in this country. Patrick Kinnersly (1974) points out that the shift system is more disruptive to the body than continuous night work because shift work upsets the body's routine, and the body clock has not time to get adjusted to a new work/ sleep pattern before it has to change again.

The biggest incentive to work shifts is, not surprisingly, the extra premium. But as a delegate of the Transport and General Workers' Union pointed out at the TUC's Women's Conference in 1974: 'It is not as if night work opens up an exciting new prospect as far as women are concerned. It is merely exploiting them by night on the same rotten jobs that they do by day.'

The Confederation of British Industry reject the idea that women will be exploited if protective legislation is repealed, because they claim that collective bargaining will offset this danger. This however ignores the fact that women in general are poorly organized. 'The ideal situation,' said Ms V. Gill of the AUEW, 'for the boss is to have us working round the clock on excessive overtime, and women are the most vulnerable people in this kind of situation. If this kind of working is the order of the day, and there is no law preventing it, then women will be pressurised into it. In the less organised factories it will be a question of "If you don't like it, there's the door".' (Women's TUC Conference, 1974).

The unions say that there has to be legislation to help women who can't help themselves. And as long as women have the extra burden of domestic responsibilities, the present legislation is in line with the realities of family life. But for the women who do have a strong union organization behind them, there is some real resentment that they are still unable to work when they like, and for as long as it suits them.

Health

Many jobs are potentially dangerous to the health and welfare of both men and women workers. But some jobs are more dangerous to women for two reasons. First, women are less strong than men, and second they have babies.

Women's relative lack of strength has often provided an easy explanation for women's subordination. But it has not usually protected them from exploitation. 'For far from woman's *physical* weakness removing her from productive work, her *social* weakness has ... evidently made her the major slave of it' (Mitchell 1971:104). It was once thought that automation would provide a panacea, that women would be liberated because the need for strenuous, physical work would end. But automation has not eliminated the harshness of much industrial work for men or women.

Women are on average 85 per cent as heavy as men. They are generally smaller, have a lesser lung capacity, and are not as strong as men in lifting, holding, pushing, pulling, or gripping. This would suggest that the level at which heavy, tiring work becomes injurious to women is lower than that for men. In only three industries, potteries, wool textiles, and jute spinning, however, have weight limits been set for women. For example, in jute spinning, the maximum weight that women may carry is 65 lb., if it is a 'compact' body, and 50 lb. if it is not compact. For other industries, the law is vague: 'A person shall not be employed to lift, carry or move any load so heavy as to be likely to cause him injury.'

Legislation to protect workers against health hazards is embodied in the *Health and Safety at Work Act*, 1975, drawn up largely on the recommendations of the Robens Report (1972). The Act gives broad guidelines as to the duties of employers and employees in matters of safety. It will work alongside existing legislation, but it is an 'enabling' Act which means that a Minister of State, on the recommendation of the newly established Health and Safety Commission, can make regulations without recourse to Parliament. What the new Act will do for women is, as yet, unknown. Past practices, however, indicate that for occupational health purposes male and female workers are classified, with a few exceptions, as one.

For example, the 'safe' level of air contamination has been determined for over 500 toxic substances. This safety limit is known as the 'threshold limit value', or TLV, and is the level to which workers may safely be exposed to toxic substances day after day. In Britain, TLVs are not legally binding, but more important perhaps is that 'much of the evidence for TLVs is based on short-term, acute exposure and/or subjective sloppily compiled "medical evidence"' (Tattersall 1975 : 18). The research that has been done on TLV levels has been on male workers, based on an average 70 kilo male, but set for male and female workers alike. This means that no allowance has been made to take account of women's smaller lung capacity or their child-bearing capabilities.

The vulnerability of pregnant women to certain poisons is not a startling new discovery. Lead, for example, has been known to be an abortive agent since the nineteenth century (women took pills containing lead to induce miscarriages). 'Females contract lead poisoning more readily, more acutely, suffer more severely, succumb to it quicker,' wrote Thomas Oliver in his book

Dangerous Trades, which was an early look at the hazards of work, in 1902. This was just four years after women had been banned from working with white lead, and present-day Factory Acts have extended the protection of women working with lead further. Women are not allowed to paint buildings with lead paint, to be employed in furnace work for the reduction or treatment of lead or ashes containing lead, or the delivering of lead. They are also restricted from working with india rubber, in the manufacture of paints and colours and in certain processes in the pottery industries.

However, apart from this umbrella legislation, no legislation specifically protects the pregnant woman, despite the fact that during this period, her body is undergoing considerable change. Anna Baetjer, author of a sympathetic and balanced book on *Women in Industry*, states:

'Although there is no evidence at present to indicate that non-pregnant women are especially susceptible to the toxic substances encountered in their occupations, pregnant women present a different problem. During pregnancy an additional burden is placed on every organ in the body as a result of the metabolic alterations and the mechanical pressures. The ability of the tissues to balance injury with repair may be considerably altered. It would seem that any chemical substance which is capable of producing a harmful effect on the internal systems of the body would be of greater danger under these conditions.' (Baetjer 1948:152)

It is not work itself that causes abortion or damage to the foetus. 'There is ... no reason why pregnant women, if their condition is satisfactory, should not perform certain types of work equally and as efficiently as normal women, if the conditions of their work are properly controlled' (Baetjer 1948:182). And to argue against this would effectively ban pregnant women from working at all.

What is a matter for concern is the number of working situations that may put women at risk. Women who work with chemicals, rubber, plastics, insecticides, anaesthetics, in laboratories, and hospitals are all in potentially hazardous environments. In one American study on women nurses, the anaesthetics used in operating theatres were thought to have caused an increase in birth defects and miscarriages (Yager 1973:724).

147

Other hospital workers, such as laboratory technicians, may come into contact with infectious agents such as measles, infectious hepatitis, viral pneumonia – all these have been associated with malformation in babies.

The dangers of some hazardous substances have of course been recognized. But for the most part workers – both men and women – live in ignorance, factory doctors have little time, employers still find it easy to overlook occupational health, and unions may find their workers threatened with redundancy if they demand employers to tighten up on safety measures.

The solution to combating the health risks of women at work is not to prohibit women from working in potentially hazardous jobs or to sack pregnant women. As the Factory Acts have sometimes been interpreted as a method of discriminating against women, so have employers' policies towards pregnant women or women or child-bearing age. In a case to be heard before the Ontario Human Rights Commission, four women workers at a General Motors of Canada factory were transferred from their jobs in 1976 because the company classified them as capable of bearing children. The employers said the switches were made because research showed that lead oxide emissions could cause miscarriages or birth defects. The women argued that they should have the right to risk exposure to lead oxide even during pregnancy.

The fears of women that they are being refused equality of opportunity because they are women could be eradicated if threshold danger levels were keyed to women and not to the 'average' male. This would doubly protect men, and with effective enforcement procedures, safeguard the health of all workers.

Pensions

Much of the thinking behind who gets what sort of pension has been based on the idea that a married woman is financially dependent on her husband. Thus, if she works outside the home, it is for pin money. When she retires she will be provided for by her husband, and if she is widowed she will live off her dead husband's pension. That 60 per cent of elderly widows are now living off social security suggests – and the Government now admits this – that the past pensions schemes for women – both

National Insurance and Occupational Pensions – have been unsatisfactory.

The growing numbers of women who now work outside the home, one in five of whom are the sole family breadwinner, together with the changing role of women, have highlighted the inequalities of the pension system. Few women, especially the married ones, have had an adequate pension. This is mainly because they paid less in contributions, over fewer years, a fact determined by their commitment to raising a family.

The new *Social Security Pensions Act*, unveiled by Barbara Castle, then Secretary of State for Social Security, in February 1975, will go a long way to improving women's pension rights, and for the first time will recognize the contribution women make to society inside and outside the home. 'It is no longer tolerable', said Mrs Castle, 'to treat women as second-class citizens entitled to third-class benefits'. The new legislation becomes operative in April 1978.

In Britain pensions fall into two parts: the State pension and the private occupational schemes. On both sides, women and the low-paid (who are mostly women anyway) have lost out. Until the introduction of the recent Act, only single women have been treated in the same way as men for the basic State pension, provided they have paid the correct number of National Insurance stamps during their working life.

However, the married woman has not had an equal return from the State. If a married woman chose to pay her National Insurance contributions in full, but then discovered that she paid in less than her husband she forfeited her own pension and claimed a married woman's pension through her husband. Her own contributions were wasted. But the married couple's pension is still not twice a single person's pension. A single person receives £15·30 (1977), but a married couple receives only £24·50 if the woman claims on her husband's contribution.

Only if a married woman paid full contributions for all her working life would she get the same pension as a single woman, and then only if she hurdled the often iniquitous 'half-test' rule. This stipulated that a woman had to pay stamps over at least half the years between her marriage and her sixtieth birthday. This hit particularly hard the woman who married fairly late – having worked up to her marriage – and then worked only for a short period after marriage.

To redress this situation, at least in part, married women have had the option of paying a reduced contribution. If a woman chose to do this (three out of four married women did), she lost the right to claim unemployment and sickness benefit. But the catch was that even if she paid the full contribution she could only claim a lower-rate on these short-term benefits. Once again, it was assumed that a married woman was provided for by her husband, and that money lost through illness or unemployment was not a crucial part of the family budget.

Attempts to redress some of the inequalities in the pensions system have again and again come up against the problem that men and women retire at different ages. Most men retire at sixty-five, while women normally do so at sixty. This age limit was set in 1940 when it was argued that women would be more likely to take up jobs outside the home (in wartime female labour was desperately needed), if five years were docked from their working life. Another reason given for the different retirement ages was that with a then average difference of five years between the ages of married couples, it was thought both unfair that a woman should work on while her husband was in retirement, and, from the husband's point of view, hard that he should have to manage the home when his wife was out at work.

The 1940 legislation has remained, and the new *Social Security Pensions Act* left the different ages unchanged. It was decided that it would be too expensive (an estimated £1,400 million) to lower the male retirement age to sixty, and that it would be unfair to raise the women's retirement age to sixty-five. As Barbara Castle generously put it: 'The lower retirement age was some compensation for the lower wages women had been drawing for years. Many women have been exploited and paid merely sweated wages' (Second Reading, the Social Security Pensions Bill, March 18, 1976).

In practice, women's lower retirement age has given employers and Government the opportunity to pay women less in pensions because it has to be spread over a longer period than for men. And again, women tend to live longer than men: for those who survive until retirement, women live on average three years longer. So for a longer life span, women are penalized for a second time. The money has to be spread over a longer period at the beginning and up to the end of their lives.

'Alas, it is a sad fact of life that equal treatment of women in the sense of equal pensions is not equality in the eyes of the actuary. Women live longer and will therefore get more in pensions in total even if the yearly payment is the same as the man's. And of course, they retire earlier which means both the pension is paid sooner, and that they have paid less towards it.'
(Richard Redden writing in the *Guardian*, March 26, 1975)

Although retirement ages have not been rationalized in the *Social Security Pensions Act*, the Act has gone further than any other pensions legislation to ensure that women get a better deal. The theory behind the Act is that for 'equal responsibilities' at work and in the home, women will receive 'equal rights'. The half-test will be abolished; the married woman's option to pay a reduced contribution has already been phased out. Up until 1976, married women could choose whether to continue to pay a reduced contribution. Those who chose to 'opt in' and to pay in full receive the full benefits that single women have enjoyed.

One of the most important features of the Act is that, for the first time, the work many women do in bringing up a family or caring for elderly relatives, will at last be recognized. The earnings related State scheme, which provides the pension paid over and above the basic, will be based on the best twenty years' earnings in a person's working life. This device is fairly flexible because the twenty years can be selected from any time during a man or woman's career (starting from 1978), and not necessarily in consecutive years. This will be a great help to working women with families who may drop out of the work force while their children are young.

Thus the time that women spend looking after dependants will be seen as acceptable ground for absence from work, and entitlements to pension benefits will not be affected. However, there is a hidden drawback : if a woman is absent from work on these 'legitimate' grounds, she will only be credited for a pension at the basic level.

Enforcement will not be that simple. Mike Brown, Information and Research Manager for the Company Pensions Information Centre, feels that 'the problem for government is to find a definition of acceptable absence from work.' One Conservative MP at the Committee stage of the new Act commented that a woman could space her children out over many years and still come into an acceptable category for absence. This, perhaps, would not be thought to be 'playing the game'.

For widows and widowers the changes that the new Act brings will not be so fundamental. A widowed mother or a widow over fifty can inherit 100 per cent of the earnings-related pensions that her husband earned, and claim an additional pension that she has earned through her own contribution, although this is subject to the maximum pension payable on one person's record. However, this ruling does not apply equally to widowers. These men will only be allowed to claim an earnings-related pension earned by their wife, if they are over retirement age, or too sick or disabled to work when their wife dies.

The new State scheme, with its increased benefits for women, is, however, only one half of the pensions tangle. As in the past, the Act relies too on occupation or company pensions schemes. These are alternatives to the State earnings-related scheme by which a company that has satisfied the Government that its own scheme is as good or as better than the State scheme can 'contract out' its employees from the State scheme. A third alternative is to use the company scheme to 'live on top' of the new State scheme.

Up until now women have fared pretty badly in the private pensions schemes. Few have been eligible and even fewer have been treated as well as men. In 1971 only 28 per cent of all working women were in an occupational pensions scheme. A woman manual worker has even less of a chance than a non-manual female worker to be eligible. Among non-manual workers, 87 per cent of men but only 56 per cent of women were covered; and among manual workers the figures were 56 per cent for men compared to 18 per cent for women (Government Actuary 1971).

These differences can be largely explained by the criteria that employers use for eligibility into their pension schemes. Two of the most common entry conditions with different requirements for men and women are related to age and length of service. Men may become eligible at 21, while women have to wait until they are 25. A study made by the General and Municipal Workers' Union, one of the few unions who have looked into company pensions practice, estimated that nearly 30 per cent of schemes discriminated in this way. The waiting period stipulation excludes many women by demanding a longer length of service, normally five years, than for men who may become eligible after one year.

These practices are defended because it is claimed that women change their employment more often than men, and that young women leave work to get married after only a short period in employment. Admittedly, women themselves have often been reluctant to join a pension scheme because they intend to marry and raise a family. However this argument is becoming less and less tenable now that more married women work outside the home.

Many women are excluded from private pension schemes because they either earn too little or only work part-time. In 1971 only 5 per cent of part-time women workers (who are one third of the female work force) were covered by an occupational pensions scheme.

The *Social Security Pensions Act* will, in theory, outlaw such discrimination against women. The paucity of statistics relating to discrimination practices spurred the Government to investigate further, and in 1975 the Occupational Pensions Board was asked to collect and submit evidence on present practice, and to make recommendations for change. When the Board reported in August 1976 its demands were modest. It felt unable to recommend legislative changes to enforce strict equality because of the problem of the different retirement age of women and men. It did, however, suggest some voluntary changes should be made. For example, that women should not be forced to retire before men and that mortality differences between men and women should be ignored in respect of pension accrual rates and in calculating lump sum benefits.

The basic requirements of the Act in respect of company pensions is that 'Women must be admitted ... on the same basis as men doing comparable work, at the same entry age, after the same period of qualifying employment and on the same basis of compulsion and choice' (Nobel Lowndes 1975).

However, the concept of 'comparable work' provides the same loopholes as exist in the *Equal Pay Act*, so this will mean that large sections of women workers will still find themselves outside an occupational pensions scheme. Mike Brown can envisage another reason why women will not become eligible. 'The Government could come unstuck here if they are making the assumption that employers will broaden female eligibility to match male eligibility. Employers may just tighten requirements of age and 'waiting period of all employees'.

Employers who decide to contract out of the State earnings-related scheme will find it expensive if they have to offer women equal entry conditions to men. 'Remembering that the commercial cost of providing a given amount of pension for a woman from the age of 60 is higher than for a man from the age of 65 ... contracting out is likely to prove a less attractive option where a predominantly female labour force is employed.' (Noble Lowndes 1975). Not to 'contract out' will theoretically be a disadvantage for women workers since company pension schemes tend to be better than the State scheme.

A firm with an occupational scheme will, as it has been seen, be required under the new Act to give equal access to women, but it will not be obliged to treat men and women exactly the same. For example, it will have to provide a widow's pension but not a widower's pension. Only a tiny percentage of schemes provide for widowers; indeed, until 1973 there were no provisions for tax relief for a company providing widowers' pensions. 'Despite this provision having been dropped, very few employers,' says Mike Brown, 'say that they want to provide for widowers. Most employers will say that it's not so important, and that to provide for all widowers would be unnecessary spending, and not meeting a genuine need.'

Dependants, too, are treated differently according to the sex of the employee. The GMWU's study found that 'often the children of widowers or male divorcees, where there is no wife, have special rights, while the children of unsupported mothers – and they would far more often be widows or divorcees than unmarried girls – get nothing. All the figures and surveys show that far fewer men are left alone to bring up children than are women.'

The limitations of the new Act reflect that the ideas that were fostered by Sir William Beveridge when he outlined Britain's post-war social security legislation are still much in evidence. He treated housewives as a race apart, very much as a dependant class. And the legacy of the belief that women's wages only supplement the male breadwinner are to be carried on with the *Social Security Pensions Act* of 1975, despite the important changes that have been made.

Maternity leave and pay

The idea that an employed woman who has a child should not be penalized for giving birth by being sacked, losing money, or by being demoted has only slowly come to be accepted.

In 1975 the *Employment Protection Act* gave women the legal right, for the first time, to be paid for six weeks maternity leave from their jobs and the right to return to work with the same employer in the same or a similiar job up to 29 weeks after birth of the baby, providing they have worked for the same firm for two years. The Act, some of whose maternity provisions came into effect in the spring of 1976, and whose pay provisions were scheduled to become effective in the spring of 1977, was to bring Britain more into line with Western Europe in maternity provision.

'The most striking difference between the UK and other parts of Europe is that here the law does not protect the woman's employment in any way during pregnancy, and the employer is under no obligation to keep her job open after confinement.'   (Incomes Data Services 1973)

In 1919 the International Labour Organization adopted a policy on maternity leave (revised in 1952). This says that a woman expecting a baby should be entitled to twelve weeks maternity leave, to include at least six weeks compulsory leave after confinement. However, it has, in Britain, taken both the increased interest in women's rights and the huge increase in the numbers of married women going to work outside the home to make some unions and employers recognize that pregnancy should be accommodated within a woman's working life, if the woman wants it to be.

Before the passing of the *Employment Protection Act* there was a great difference in attitude and practice towards maternity leave and pay between the public and the private sector. The public sector – local government, the Civil Service, the nationalized industries, the Post Office, the electricity, gas, and water boards, state schools, and the universities – had, on the whole, detailed maternity schemes (although women in white-collar jobs were more fully covered than women doing unskilled or manual work).

In the private sector the reverse was true, with very few

formal maternity provisions. There were a number of informal arrangements, and in some firms women took maternity leave under sick pay schemes, although maternity is hardly a medical affliction. In the private sector the distinction drawn between white-collar jobs and those done by unskilled workers was striking. Thus, Marks and Spencer Ltd allowed only senior and professional female staff maternity leave (for up to six months on half pay). Barclays Bank and Honeywell, the electronics firm, gave clerical and administrative staff up to seven months paid maternity leave in some cases, but the scheme was operated at the discretion of management. The Metal Box Company, with 9,000 hourly paid female employees, had a scheme under which women with more than five years service with the company received up to three months full pay, less National Insurance. Maternity leave was calculated against sick pay entitlement. Employees with less than five years service were eligible for unpaid maternity leave (examples quoted in Incomes Data 1973).

But even in the year before the *Employment Protection Act* institutionalized maternity provisions, many firms expected resignation or dismissal to be the proper response to a pregnant employee. One of the largest insurance companies in the country, for instance, expected women in both clerical and managerial jobs, to leave before their pregnant state became obvious.

The Women's Advisory Committee of the TUC drew up – before the employment protection legislation – a code of 'Best Practice' for the public sector, which was designed to be used by union negotiators and employers. Its main suggestions were that all full-time women employees, and some part timers, should be eligible for paid maternity leave, providing they had twelve months' continuous service; that leave should last eighteen weeks; that maternity leave should not be taken against sick pay entitlement; and that maternity pay should be made up of four weeks on full pay less National Insurance maternity benefit, plus fourteen weeks on half pay without deducting the National Insurance benefit, unless the combined total comes to more than normal full pay, where pay should be enough to bring the National Insurance benefit up to the usual wage sum.

The provisions of the *Employment Protection Act* fall far short of these suggestions. Indeed the maternity leave provisions of the Act have been criticized on a number of counts – by women's organizations and bodies like the National Council for One Parent Families – on the grounds that they do not give women enough help, and by employers' organizations on the grounds that they establish both a financial and administrative burden for industry and commerce.

But the need to establish maternity leave has not been seriously questioned. The 1971 Census showed that some 62 per cent of all female employees in Britain were married women and that 600,000 of these were mothers of children under five years old. In 1976 the Equal Opportunities Commission estimated that three and a quarter million women of child bearing age were in employment. The proportion of women in different age groups who go out to work varies, predictably, with age. Thus the 1971 Census showed that 36 per cent of married women aged 25–9 were in employment, compared to 59 per cent of married women in the 45–9 age group. However, between 1961–71 one of the largest increases in the number of married women going out to work occurred in the group aged 20–24. A variety of influences and circumstances are at work here, but the increase does show how dramatic the switch away from the automatic decision to 'stop work' on marriage or the birth of a child has been in one of the major child-bearing age groups.

The passing of the *Employment Protection Act* does not, of course, mean that present, more generous agreements in industry will be scaled down to the Act's modest requirements. Nor does it seem likely that all eligible women will take advantage of the maternity leave provisions. Miss Betty Lockwood, chairman of the EOC, said in 1976 that 'best estimates indicate that only about six and a half per cent of the female work force of child-bearing age – 221,000 women – will take up maternity pay when it comes into force in April 1977, and even fewer will take up the leave option and return to work'.

Among the reasons for this are the paucity of child care arrangements for pre-school age children in Britain, the desire of some mothers to stay at home with their babies and the fact that many women will not be acquainted with their rights under the employment protection legislation. One small survey in 1974 found that take-up rates of maternity leave were high or low depending on the attitude and encouragement or otherwise of

157

management and personnel officers. Another factor was the example set by a woman manager. 'One technical support section of a University department provided a number of maternity leave cases, and it was discovered that the section manager served as a model, and gave moral support to women who were thinking about taking maternity leave themselves' (Fonda 1976).

The major criticism of compulsory maternity leave provision from employers' organizations centred on its cost and administrative inconvenience. Because of pressure from employers the legislation was amended by the Government to provide a maternity pay fund, financed by hiving off a small percentage of the employer's National Insurance contribution into the fund. In October 1975, when the fund was announced (*Guardian* October 14, 1975) it was estimated by the Government that £25 million would be paid out by the fund in 1977. Some employers were also worried by the difficulties that they believed would arise from having to keep open a woman's job for up to twenty-nine weeks.

The National Council for One Parent Families, in a document commenting on the employment protection proposals in 1974, said that it wanted to see an eighteen-week period over which maternity benefit would be paid. In support of this proposal it pointed out that, in France, women are entitled to fourteen weeks maternity leave at 90 per cent of normal earnings under social security, that in Italy women get twenty weeks at 80 per cent of earnings paid by social security, and that in the Netherlands they receive 12–16 weeks at full pay, again covered by social security.

A number of women Labour MPs also voiced criticism of the maternity provisions of the Bill during its report stage. Jo Richardson, MP for Barking, unsuccessfully moved an amendment to change the qualifying period for maternity pay from two years to one year. She said that two years was an unrealistic and absurdly lengthy period for women, particularly manual workers, many of whom worked for short periods in a number of different jobs. It was also pointed out that the women who would fall outside the provisions of the legislation would be the most vulnerable of the female work force – the very young, and the poorest women in unskilled jobs where there is a rapid turnover of labour.

Fears, and occasionally threats, were also expressed that

maternity leave provisions would encourage employers to hire men instead of women. But Betty Lockwood said in June 1976 that the EOC would be monitoring employment statistics.

'Where it appears to the Commission that recruitment of men only is taking place, or where there is consistent replacement of women by men, this would establish a prima facie case of discriminatory policies which the Commission would need to investigate. The Commission could bring into play its power to undertake formal investigations and to issue non-discrimination notices.'

EIGHT

Trade Unions : it started with the match girls

'They climbed a flight of steps to the printing shop where, by means of copper plates, printing presses, mineral colours and transfer-papers, most of the decoration was done. The room was filled by a little crowd of people – oldish men, women and girls, divided into printers, cutters, transferrers and apprentices ... The room smelt of oil and flannel and humanity; the old women looked stern and shrewish, the pretty young women pert and defiant, the younger girls meek. The few men seemed out of place. By what trick had they crept into the very centre of that mass of femininity? It seemed wrong, scandalous, that they should remain.'

(*Anna of the Five Towns*, Arnold Bennett)

Arnold Bennett's descriptions of work in the Midland potteries at the turn of this century show, above and elsewhere in the novel, that women workers were, however skilled and occasionally comparatively well-paid, both separate from and usually subordinate to the men. This pattern of labour was an integral part of the industrial revolution and was mirrored in emerging associations and unions. To some extent, today's unions are still bound up in that legacy.

With the industrial revolution, women entered into economic competition with men as wage earners. Then, as now, some employers preferred women because they were thought to be more docile and worked for less money. Women's 'natural dexterity' was also much admired, then, as now. Employers 'finding that the child or woman was a more obedient servant to himself, and an equally efficient slave to his machinery – was disposed to displace the male adult labourer ...' (P. Gaskell, *Manufacturing Population of England*, 1833. Quoted in Pinchbeck 1969 : 188).

For the vast majority of women workers who were affected by the industrial revolution, the changing structure took them out of their homes and into the textile factories as wage earners. When weaving and spinning were done by hand, the bulk of the spinning of the yarn was done by women, and most of the weaving by men. Technology (Hargreave's spinning jenny was invented in 1764, and power looms became effective from the beginning of the nineteenth century) turned this division of labour on its head : women took over weaving in the factories where the machinery was lighter than the old handlooms, and men took over spinning, which required greater strength. There was much antipathy, both from moral-minded public bodies and from the men in industry to the presence of female factory workers, but the many women who were the wives and daughters of handloom weavers in fact kept them from starvation. According to Ivy Pinchbeck (1969) this modified some of the jealousy and dislike that the male domestic weavers might have otherwise felt for the women.

However, male workers in industry were in general afraid of the invasion of cheap, docile, female labour. In 1808, the hat makers had written into their rules a decision to exclude all women from the trade. In 1829 the Grand General Union of All Spinners passed a resolution 'that the union shall include only male spinners and piecers'. Women were urged to form a separate union. This at least was a recognition that women workers were there for good, which was more than the potters could grasp sixteen years later.

In an appeal to women starting work on the new 'flat press' machines, the potters' union pleaded 'to maidens, wives, and mothers, we say that machinery is your deadliest enemy ... it will destroy your natural claim to homes and domestic duties, and will immure you and your toiling little ones in over heated and dirty shops, there to weep and toil and pine and die' (TUC 1955:30).

The Combination Acts made trade unionism illegal between 1799 and 1824, and thereafter a combination of hostility by some craftsmen to women workers in the same trade, the diffidence of many women, and tradition, ensured that women did not join the labour movement in force until the last quarter of the nineteenth century. There were, of course, some stout exceptions. In May 1832 there was a strike of 1,500 women card setters in Peep Green, Yorkshire, for equal pay with men. They refused to set cards for less than a halfpenny a thousand. There was also some organization of women along Friendly Society lines – into societies with names like the Ancient Virgins and Female Druids – which were intended more to ensure against bad times than to be political.

There had long been a strong tradition of female membership among the weaving sections of the Lancashire cotton unions. In 1859 the North East Lancashire Amalgamated Society was formed, for both men and women, and in 1884 the Northern Counties Amalgamated Association of Weavers began, where men and women paid the same dues and received the same pay for the same work.

But by the mid century, when unions for individual crafts (the New Model unions) were being formed, women were not recruited. Thus, excluded from the mainstream of trade union activity among the industrial working classes, it was left to women to set up unions on their own.

The first step towards organizing the mass of women workers was taken in 1874 with the Women's Protective and Provident League, later to become the famous Women's Trade Union League. Mrs Emma Paterson was its moving spirit. A middle-class lady, she saw the need for a separate union organization for women after visiting the Female Umbrella Sewers Union in New York. At first the League professed some rather coy objectives: its purpose among others being,

> 'to acquire information which will enable friends of the working classes to give a more precise direction than at present to their offers of sympathy and help ... and to promote an entente cordiale between the labourer, the employer and the consumer.'   (TUC 1955:45)

Mrs Paterson was also against protective legislation for women, although later the League came out in favour of it.

The work of the League was eventually instrumental in setting up the Sweated Labour Trade Boards in the early years of the twentieth century, and it pressed for greater control over working conditions in factories. Its great contribution to the trade union movement was to alert women to the need for organization.

It had much prejudice to fight. In 1877 the Trades Union Congress, then only three years old, had declared that 'it was the duty of men and husbands to bring about a condition of things when their wives should be in their proper sphere at home instead of being dragged into competition of livelihood with the great and strong men of the world' (TUC 1955:52). In the same year, the Birmingham brass workers, who had long worked with women, refused to support the League because to organize, they said, was to recognize that those women who 'turn at the lathe and file at the vice' were permanent fixtures.

So welcome for women in the labour movement was far from being whole-hearted, and in many ways the fears of male workers have never disappeared.

But it was, after all, a women's strike that marked the beginning of the next stage of trade union development. The match girls' strike of 1889 has become justly famous, and was so at the time. The women workers at Bryant and May's East End match factory were fearfully badly paid and worked in appalling conditions – one of the hazards was 'phossy jaw', which was literally gangrene of the jaw caused by exposure to phosphorus. Conditions at the factory prompted a group of Fabians, among them Sidney Webb, Annie Besant, and Bernard Shaw, to boycott Bryant and May products and to publicize the scandal. Mrs Annie Besant's article in *Link* magazine, listing the women's grievances, triggered off militant action in 1889. These included a visit to the Bow works by a factory inspector who reported that the allegations of the women (they were fined for having dirty feet, had money stopped if they left burnt matches on benches) were true. The management reacted to the article with fury and found an excuse for sacking one of the women's leaders. Fourteen hundred women promptly came out on strike in protest. The strike became famous there and then. Leader writers (in *The Times*) denounced socialist agitators, and the *Church Times* said sourly that 'no one supposes their wages are satisfactory but their conditions are ruled by the price they can get for their work' (quoted in Stafford 1961 : 73).

If strike action was stimulated by the zeal of Annie Besant, it became a famous victory for women unionists because of the bravery of the strikers and their recognition that their only hope lay in uniting against their employers. The power of even the most miserable workers, once they combined, was not lost on the dock workers, the gas workers, and the thousands of other general labourers, who in the next decade began to form the great new general unions. These, for the first time on a national scale, recruited women on equal terms with men.

But even this new stage in unionism did not touch that major and most neglected section of female labour, the domestic servant. In 1881 the Census showed that there were over one and half million women in domestic service, which was 44 per cent of all employed women. Domestic servants had little regular free time, they were isolated from one another or, in large houses, set against each other : 'Between the lordly butler and the lowly kitchen maid, the haughty housekeeper and the urchin stableboy no bond existed which could have drawn them into alliance against the employer' (Burnett 1974 : 169). Their lot, working irregular hours in isolated situations, was not unlike that facing women in the service industries (hotels, restaurants, cleaning) today.

The few attempts to organize servants were doomed to failure. In 1872 unions were formed in Dundee and Leamington, but these soon fizzled out. The short life of the London and Provincial Domestic Servants Union was similarly ineffective though well-attended and enthusiastic meetings showed that servants felt the need for an organization of their own.

In 1907 there were 200,000 women trade unionists, according to Sidney and Beatrice Webb, where in 1890 there had been 100,000. Most of these were still however in textiles. It was one of the greatest leaders of the trade union movement, Mary Macarthur, the secretary of the National Federation of Women Workers, who swept up thousands of scattered and unprotected women workers – the Dundee jute workers, Lancashire chain workers, the jam makers and biscuit makers of the East End. By 1914, there were 437,000 women in trade unions out of a total union membership of 4,145,000 (Chief Registrar of Friendly Societies).

The two World Wars did more to bring women into the union movement than all the other events of the twentieth century. In the First World War female membership trebled in four years, while in the Second World War numbers for women in unions doubled, so that by 1943 membership was almost two million, a figure not overtaken until 1956. The wars enabled unions to build up strong organizations for both men and women. There was also a jump in male membership but this was not so dramatic – male union membership increased by 60 per cent compared to a 200 per cent increase for women.

Most women had enrolled in the big general unions during the First World War when there were few objections to their membership. The craft unions on the whole still did not welcome women. 'The small metal unions ... in despair at the ineffectual struggle against the cheap female labour, sought a compromise and tried to organise women with a view to confining them to certain branches of the trade' (Drake 1918:13).

Yet the trade union movement failed to build on the huge increase in female membership brought about by the war. In 1921 female membership stood at over a million. Two years later it had sunk to 800,000. By 1933 it was 731,000, the lowest figure of the inter-war years. Even so, this was almost double the pre-war figure. (There was a parallel decline in male membership of similarly drastic proportions over the same period.)

The post-war depression caused women to drop out of the labour market in large numbers. But they were also encouraged to go. Beatrice Webb wrote a minority report to the report by the War Cabinet Committee on Women in Industry. She felt that the Committee had assumed that industry was a male prerogative and had therefore not looked at women's wages as they should have been looked at, in relation to men's. Then, a conference held in 1918 on the position of women in industry, between trade unions and employers in the Bristol area, gives an idea of the reluctance to accept women as equal in industrial rights to men. A resolution stated grandly, 'that women should, as a matter of course, relinquish the jobs in which they have replaced men ... so long as men are available to fill them'.

Since the Second World War it has been women workers who have provided the largest recruitment source for trade unions. Today, over a quarter of the membership of the Trade Union Congress is female (2,772,000 women out of a total of 10,250,000), and in the past two decades almost two thirds of the new members have been women. One reason for this – apart from the speed with which some unions recognized the membership potential of female labour – was the post-war mushrooming of local and national government departments, the boom in office work, and the creation of the National Health Service.

The National Union of Public Employees (NUPE), which now contains more women members than any other union, including the large general unions like the General and Municipal Workers Union (GMWU), which used to have the largest female membership, is a perfect example. Between 1950 and 1974 NUPE's female membership shot up from 40,000 to 321,302, an increase in the *percentage* of women from 24 per cent to 63 per cent. The Confederation of Health Service Employees (COHSE), the Association of Professional, Executive, Clerical and Computer Staff (APEX) and civil services unions like the Civil and Public Servants Association (CPSE) have all capitalized on burgeoning female employment in white-collar jobs. On the other hand, unions catering for areas of traditional female employment like hosiery, dyeing and bleaching, weaving and jute, textiles and garment-making have seen their memberships decline or at least stagnate, although in percentage terms women still dominate unions like the National Union of Hosiery and Knitwear Workers (NUHKW) and the National Union of Tailors and Garment Workers (NUTGW). In the latter union women formed 86 per cent of the membership in 1974.

But women do not become union executive members or full-time officials in the numbers that their general membership warrants. Several reasons for this are put forward by concerned trade unionists and one of the obvious ones is that the majority of women workers are married and find that family responsibilities conflict with union work. Even the way a marriage is run can prevent women's participation in the union. 'About 80 or 90 per cent of my women are married. They say the money's grand and so they're not prepared to rock the boat. The vociferous ones are the single ones. The married ones just say I'll go and ask "him"' (Hattie Brierlay, General and Municipal Workers Union shop steward in a Newcastle sweet factory).

The time and place of union branch meetings is also the subject of habitual complaint when meetings are held out of working hours and off the workplace. Three women shop stewards in the engineering union, Associated Union of Engineering Workers (AUEW), in a South London electronics factory, said that despite being officials, they never went to branch meetings because of travelling and family responsibilities. But then there appeared also to be a deeper motive. Mrs Stella Morris: 'The women are interested in nothing else than being happy at work, and we know that we can always go to the men if there's a problem we can't deal with in our section.'

The same tendency to abdicate responsibility – a product of granite-hard traditions – was noted by Joe Mills, regional group secretary of the Transport and General Workers Union (TGWU) in the North-East of England. 'There are a number of places where women are becoming shop stewards but that's about the limit of their involvement. Only a few go on. What stops them is where there is a mixed work force. There's a tendency to let the men get on with it.'

A survey by NALGO, the local government officers union, found that 92 per cent of all branch meetings were held outside working hours. Few branches had arrangements for child care at meetings. The results of this were mirrored predictably enough, in the proportion of women holding office in NALGO.

'In the largest individual service, local government, 40·7 per cent of the membership are female but only 17·2 per cent of executive committee members are women ... Posts like assistant secretary are presumably held by women so that they can do the branch typing work. 41·5 per cent of assistant secretaries are female but only 5·3 per cent of chairmen.'

(NALGO 1975:30)

The lack of women in executive positions is common to all unions at all levels. The TUC general council has thirty-seven members of whom two are women (1976 figures), but both of these fill reserved seats and are not elected alongside the men. There are no women general secretaries of any of the large unions, although smaller unions in the traditional female industries have, in some cases, a long record of women officials. Margaret Fenwick is the general secretary of the Union of Jute, Flax and Kindred Textile Operatives. 'We've had women presidents since the 1920s and since 1911 we've had a committee of management of whom the rule book says eight should be women if at all possible, and usually we get near it.'

The Bolton Weavers Association has a declining female membership – it now stands at 51 per cent of the total of 40,000 members – although the union is more or less run by women. Miss Hilda Unsworth, the association's general secretary says cheerfully: 'We have four women on the staff here. We have had men, in the past, but death or dishonesty have taken them all away. To have an all woman staff, that's unique now isn't it. We're as efficient and probably better than most.'

There has been a continuing debate, since the Women's Protective and Provident League was set up in 1874, among women trade unionists about the wisdom of separatism – of having separate unions and sections of unions for women members. At the end of the First World War the million women trade unionists were organized in 383 trade unions, of which thirty-six were all-female associations. The National Federation of Women Workers, founded in 1906, and with 60,000 members in 1919 was politically the most effective of the women's unions. And its secretary, Mary Macarthur, urged women to join appropriate unions, whether mixed or separate. But she was anxious to prevent women being submerged in largely male unions. The report of the Joint Committee of Industrial Women's Organisations of 1918, under the chairmanship of Mary Macarthur, demanded:

'Special provision should be made in the rules for the representation of women on the governing bodies of the unions, and there should be inside each trade union special machinery for dealing with the organisation of women in the trade with their special needs and grievances.'

(Quoted in Rowbotham 1973:118)

The realization that women workers had special needs that were often neglected by trade unions led to the setting up of the first TUC women's conference in 1931. The conference, which is held annually, has been used to debate issues that might not get an airing in any mixed forum. Resolutions are passed on to the general council of the TUC although it need take no notice of them, and frequently does not. In 1975 the women's conference resolved that the representation of Group 19 (women workers) should be increased from two seats to three on the general council. The general council disagreed, although it did suggest that ways should be considered of increasing women's representation – which was what the women's conference had said in the first place.

Supporters of the women's conference say that it acts as a training ground for women trade unionists, that it 'draws them out', and that it encourages solidarity. Opponents say this is condescending, and the separate conference was described in 1974, in a debate at the annual conference of the TUC on the motion to abolish the women's conference, as 'sexual apartheid'. A delegate from the Society of Civil Servants said : 'We believe that the Women's TUC in the long run discourages full and active participation by women in the broader trade union movement because it gives the impression that their problems are on the periphery of our thinking.'

Opponents of womens' committees, the appointment of women's officers, and the publication of pamphlets aimed at women workers – all of which have been set up by certain unions since the emergence of the Women's Movement – say a special concentration on women is a divisive force in trade unionism. However, unions are not, and never have been, homogeneous : they have been built on differentials and organized around sectional differences – skilled and unskilled, manual and white-collar, male and female.

The need for greater participation and representation of women at all levels of union activity is not disputed – but the methods of how best to achieve this are. The TUC, which has a woman's officer, is conscious that women are under-represented as officers and office bearers within unions. In a questionnaire sent out to unions in 1975, answers from sixty-two unions showed that there were only seventy-one full-time women officials compared to 2,259 males (*Financial Times*, November 10, 1975). The TUC has also recognized the existence of discrimination against women within the union movement by drawing up an equal opportunities clause to be included in labour agreements. The clause says that parties to the agreement will 'promote equal opportunity in employment regardless of workers' sex, marital status, creed, colour, race or ethnic origin'.

And within individual unions there is recognition that women have been neglected.

'It would be easy, but not very constructive, to dwell on the singular lack of progress we have made. What is important is that belated though it is, unions do now recognise that their women members have been shamefully neglected and many of them are genuinely trying to make up for lost time. Their new-found interest is not merely altruistic. Women constitute a majority in several large unions and there are increasing signs that they are questioning why the goods haven't been delivered.' (TASS 1975)

The ability and willingness of trade unions to better the opportunities for women at work and to encourage greater participation in union organization vary. They depend on factors such as the size of female membership, the homogenity or otherwise of a union's membership, and the type of work done by most women members.

A union like the Union of Shop, Distributive and Allied Workers (USDAW), for example, faces difficulties organizing women shop workers – many of whom earn very low wages. Most shops have less than five employees, so that actually reaching potential members is an enormous problem. USDAW does well in negotiation with multiples – in 1974 assistants in Woolworth's won what was then seen as an amazing breakthrough when their basic weekly wage was raised to £30 a week through an USDAW agreement – but it cannot do what it would like to for the women working in the local baker's or chemist's shop. The membership of USDAW is around 350,000 and a third of these drop out and are replaced each year. The union therefore often has to run to stand still. This is also true of the National Union of Tailors and Garment Workers whose turnover is high, and which covers a labour-intensive work force that is widely scattered.

But a rapid turnover of members does not, by itself, mean that the involvement of women in the union cannot be increased. The National Union of Public Employees loses roughly a third of its members each year. It has also had to deal with a ten-fold growth in ten years, and many of its women members are part-time, working in the school meals service, or as hospital or civil service cleaners. But it manages to draw in a much higher proportion of women than other, similar unions.

NUPE, according to its deputy general secretary Bernard Dix, does not want to pretend that altering the union structure will do away with the problems women face. But in 1975 the union reorganized its general council to allow for five women's seats out of twenty-six. 'We had this problem that the overwhelming majority of our women members are part time – we could get them active at the workplace but that was about all. So we decided on positive discrimination' (Bernard Dix). The five seats, which can only be occupied by women, are voted on at the same time as the other seats on the executive.

But in NUPE, as in most unions, there is still a massive under-representation of women both as full-time officers of the union (in 1975 there was only one woman among 140 paid officers) and as officials at every stage. NUPE has run day release courses for training shop stewards, but they were not popular with many women who might have been interested because they last one whole day every week, which interferes with family life. So in 1976, NUPE's London division began a pilot scheme for shop-steward training, which lasted a half day every week for twenty weeks and which was only open to women. This slight adjustment did the trick and attracted a number of potential women shop stewards.

There are still far too few women shop stewards throughout the trade union movement. The job of stewards cannot be underestimated particularly in their role of making members aware of the *Equal Pay Act* and the *Sex Discrimination Act*. Women shop stewards also play an important part in showing new women members that trade unionism is not an exclusive male club. However, even NUPE is not immune to sexist pre-conceptions. The union believes that it is unlikely that large numbers of women will be attracted to the ranks of the paid officers. Bernard Dix:

'By the time a woman is able to do the travelling and the irregular hours that the job of officer entails, she is likely to be in her forties with her family grown up. And what woman of

171

that age is going to want to dash about the country. And what union will want someone of that age?'

Much of the commitment to improving the position of women in the trade union movement has come from the white-collar unions that organize in the public sector and in offices. The Association of Scientific, Technical and Managerial Staffs (ASTMS) has 300,000 members of whom about 60,000 are women. Members of the Women's Movement within the union pressed for, and got, a separate National Women's Advisory Council, in 1975, to which the union divisions will nominate members. This decision, which sprang from a series of work-shops and conferences on how the position of women could best be improved within ASTMS, was not well received by everyone in the union. Muriel Turner, the union's finance officer and assistant general secretary said:

'I take the view very strongly that if you separate, or form a women's committee, then the executive when it's con-fronted with a women's issue, will just say, "Oh, refer it to the women's committee" rather than saying, it's our problem, let's press the Minister on it or whatever.'

NALGO, the local government officers' union, wrestled with the same problem. But the report from its equal rights working party rejected the idea of special womens' seats on the executive because, it said, members should represent all members, and it likewise rejected having a special NALGO women's conference. But it did recommend having a national union committee to monitor discrimination within the union, and in agreements with employers and it called for an education programme 'to transform membership attitudes and to make the union aware that discrimination against women is a trade union issue re-quiring a trade union response' (NALGO 1975:32).

Union action to improve the conditions of work for women members need not only benefit women. A drive against low pay will tend to benefit a higher proportion of women than men but can be easily accepted by men not sympathetic to women's issues. Fighting for equal pay in some cases produces rises for men as well as women and those unions with large female memberships are usually aware of having to take the men with them in pursuit of female equality. Ray Edwards, assistant general secretary of the Association of Professional, Executive, Clerical and Computer Staff (APEX), which has 54 per cent female membership, was particularly active in encouraging members to be militant in demanding equal pay. APEX backed a number of equal pay strikes in the run up to the final stage of the *Equal Pay Act* in 1975. Ray Edwards was conscious that the male membership had to be accommodated as well.

'I've always argued that protection is one of trade union-ism's primary functions and that therefore no one should work below the rate, and that if you stop people having to work below the rate then that will strengthen trade unionism. In 17 years of union work one of my biggest embarrassments has been seeing members decide to strike, go out, suffer and then settle and then seeing the men get two quid and the women, who had suffered equally, get one. But in the 30 or so equal pay strikes we've had there hasn't been any mass counter reaction by the men – I think because of the way we approached it. We said, "how many of you can put your hand on your heart and say that your standard of living doesn't depend on what your wife brings home". And in many areas we've been able to show how cheap labour works against men. We've pointed to specific jobs where women walked into posts, getting the edge on men, because they were cheaper.'

It is not always so amiable. Muriel Turner of ASTMS:

'We have a firm policy that we will not have the women going out of jobs first if it's a question of redundancies. People are people and they all can have family commitments. We had a conference though in the Midlands which has been badly hit by recession and most of the audience were men from industry and we had a lot of questions on the lines of "Why keep women in jobs when men are losing theirs?" Our policy didn't go down altogether well.'

The view of the man as rightful breadwinner and so the true unionist has tended to exclude women from enjoying full acceptance in unions. The mystique of a kind of male brother-hood is a strong feature of union history. Drinking, for example, once gave workers access to jobs because pubs were primitive labour exchanges, with the publican acting as go-between with

173

the employer. Then there were 'footings', drinking times when a new apprentice was welcomed into the craft. And again, drinking was part of the celebrations of 'shop' outings. Not to participate in drinking marked a man off as an odd sort of workmate. Women are still notably absent from this kind of camaraderie.

Women may not feel they belong, they may feel oppressed because they are not automatically accepted and are not given a sympathetic ear. 'When I get up and speak my heart's going like the clappers, but they're thinking "Look at that brazen bitch" ' (Hattie Brierlay, GMWU shop steward). An outspoken woman is a matter for comment because there is a tendency for men to believe that 'women are no bloody good – they'll accept anything'.

Women feature in far fewer strikes than men do. The Donovan Commission on Trade Unions and Employers' Associations reported in 1968 that the four industries in Britain that consistently showed the highest strike record, both in terms of stoppages and days lost, were coal-mining, docks, shipbuilding, and motor vehicle manufacturing. All these industries have a predominantly male workforce with a tradition of strong union activity.

Many of the occupations with a low strike record – catering, clothing, footwear, the distributive trades, service industries – have a female dominated workforce and a weak record of unionism. Other features of working life that have been linked with a low level of industrial action – small firms organized on patriarchal lines, a scattered workforce unable to express common interests, and unsophisticated technology – are all typical of many women's working conditions.

The most immediate reason for women's rare involvement in strike activity is that only one in four women belong to trade unions. And it is unionization that makes strikes possible. Without union organization workers do not band together collectively to pursue a common interest and the strongest card that unorganized workers have to play is to hand in their notice. (It is instructive to note that a high turnover in a particular industry is associated with a low strike record.)

However, women do go on strike, and at least one all-women's strike, notably that of the Bryant & May matchgirls made trade-union history. More recently, the rise in female union membership, the campaign for women's equality, and a recognition of women's oppression, even among working-class women, have helped women recognize their potential strength at work.

Even so, women are not drawn into strikes as easily as men. 'I believe women are more responsible than men – they have the bills to pay, a financial obligation towards their families. Women stop to think about the implications of a strike, they are not so spontaneous as men', said Elizabeth Costley, appointed officer of the General and Municipal Workers' Union with responsibility for education in the northern region. Women's reluctance to strike is, in part, a reflection of their loyalty to the home, which they put before their work. It is also part of their political inexperience. 'Women don't know their capabilities,' said shop steward Hattie Brierlay. 'When I began to look after the canteen girls at the factory they were grossly underpaid. After 10 weeks of fighting for them I told them to tell me when dinner was ready and then come and sit down. They got their rise after this brief strike, but I instigated it. They didn't ask me. I said that a strike was the only solution. There were a few faint hearts but they all came out.'

Support from union officials and fellow male workers is often sadly lacking when women strike. The women strikers at a small engineering factory in Derbyshire in 1975 felt that support from the AUEW was only luke warm (BBC TV 'We're women but we're workers', *Man Alive*, June 26, 1975). 'Because we're a load of women they look at you and say "what are you doing there" ... If it was a man's strike they'd all be there', said one woman striker, distressed by the men's condescending attitude. Male support is not expected by women, but it is welcomed. 'You don't know what it felt like that Monday, when we stood out on the picket lines on our own, and then the men came out. I could have hugged every one of them' (woman AUEW (Tass) member in an equal pay strike at an Ipswich engineering firm).

Another strike, at Salford Electric Instruments in Heywood, Lancashire started when the women demanded bonuses equal to those earned by men. It was not supported by male workers. 'We are feeling bitter about it', said Bella Fullard, shop steward. 'The union is backing us but only two or three men at the factory are supporting us. We are absolutely disgusted with them' (*Guardian* October 1, 1974). This was the first sign of women's militancy at the factory and the women felt that they had been let down, but, according to the *Guardian* report (October 10, 1974): 'There seems to be a feeling among the men that the women, though playing with commendable enthusiasm, just don't understand the rules of the game.' After the strike was over – it lasted for ten weeks – women who had taken part in it said that the results were threefold.

'The main thing was that it united the women workers in the factory which was something the union had been trying to do for five years. That unity is still there and I think the management would have second thoughts about taking on the girls again. Then I don't think the women will be as timid and quiet again as they were before and you can see how they're not shouted at and bullied like they were before. And the third thing is that the men – who didn't join us – were treated with utter contempt by the women and there's still a lot of suspicion.'

(Mrs Julie Lomas, former AUEW shop steward at
the factory; authors' interview)

The most famous recent women's strike was at Ford's (Dagenham) in 1968 when 187 sewing machinists pursued a three-week strike that ended in victory and lost Ford's £8 million of export orders. The strike was a clear indication to other women workers that women did have economic strength and could use it to their advantage. This was prophetically, if nervously, noted by officials at the Department of Employment at the time.

The strike began when the women's demand to be up-graded, which would have given them an increase of 5d an hour, was turned down by the management. They were soon joined by nearly 200 women from Ford's Halewood plant. The issue was blurred by the fact that there was no union strike procedure to make grading grounds for an official strike, so at first the unions were unwilling to intervene. When the AUEW did take up the fight it was put to their executive that the strike was over equal pay and not grading. The women felt that it was a bit of both – they had been put in an unduly low grade because theirs was predominantly a woman's job. The strike was eventually settled after the intervention of Barbara Castle, then Secretary of State for Employment and Productivity, 'over a cup of tea' as it was cosily reported. The women machinists did not get re-graded, but they achieved a 7d an hour increase, which took them from 87 per cent to 92 per cent of the men's rate. In a speech, Mrs Castle said: 'Let us salute those lasses. They were determined not to give in, although they were desperately hard up and family lives were almost broken up.'

Taking up issues like equal pay, unfair job evaluation schemes, and lack of promotion prospects is not always seen by unions as being a dose of nasty medicine. It has the effect of making women more involved in the union, keener to work for it, and it can increase membership. Ray Edwards said that the equal pay issue doubled up as a membership drive for APEX. 'It's a commonplace that union membership drops when there is any kind of pay policy by the Government, but during the last one (the Conservative's Wage Control Policy) we picked up a number of previously unorganised companies and membership of the union increased by around 20 per cent.'

ASTMS, too, found that an issue like that of equal pay was a good advertisement for the benefits of joining a union. Muriel Turner:

'One of the problems in our particular field is that equal pay is there on the surface so it's formally not a problem. The problem is low pay. Last year [1974] we ran a specific low pay campaign, we said that no adult employee should earn less than £30 a week. We took on one or two companies where people did earn less than that and they were mostly women. We went to the Royal Liver Buildings in Liverpool – where the Liver Birds work on TV – and we marched round and round the building with placards. We closed the building in fact and got what we wanted, people were hanging out of windows and it caused a stir. It was propaganda and we got the increases and the girls were tickled pink, some of them had huge increases.'

It is noticeable that the unions with a homogeneous base have tended to tackle the problems of their women members with greater vigour than have the larger general unions, where the bargaining power of women is less. Thus the Tobacco Workers Union (21,000 members of whom 16,000 are women) dealing with only a few large employers, managed to negotiate relatively good rates of pay for women workers, which meant that a number of men got rises as well. Furthermore the union agreed with management's guidelines for achieving greater equality of opportunity between men and women. This included a clause saying that recruitment should be operated so that there was no reduction in the proportion of women employed. The employers tried to get women to do night shift as an exchange, but the union refused to agree to this.

The Association of Teachers in Technical Institutions is another union with a uniform base, although it has only 8,000 women out of a total membership of 55,000. ATTI devoted some thought to the needs of its women members and in 1974 it carried out a 10 per cent sample of women members. This found that many women believed that promotion was denied them because of their sex, that interview procedures were biased against them, that a very small proportion scaled the career ladder, and that where they were heads of departments it was mostly in domestic science, secretarial, and office work.

In response to the worries expressed by respondents in the survey, the Association decided to press colleges to allow the results of interviews and appointments to be monitored perhaps by having staff members on the committee which approves appointments. But ATTI was also concerned that few women bring cases of alleged discrimination before the association; although the survey suggests that a strong belief in discrimination exists.

The women's rights debate which became vigorous in the early 1970s within the trade union movement, has varied in strength and influence from union to union. The lack of commitment to gaining equality for women, at one end of the spectrum, was best symbolized by the National Graphical Association which – in International Women's Year – instructed members that the *Sex Discrimination Act* should make no difference to the union's determination to keep women out of the composing rooms. At the other end a great deal of research has gone into the pay, promotion prospects, training, and representation in unions like TASS, APEX, ASTMS, NALGO, and NUT.

A campaign to extend the traditional interests of unions to encompass issues of particular interest to women – nursery provision, abortion, contraception, and family allowances – was launched in March 1974. The Working Women's Charter lists ten aims and in its first eighteen months of existence it attracted the support of twelve unions at their national conferences. The

Charter's aims were debated at the 1975 TUC Congress but conference voted against adopting them by 6,224,000 to 3,697,000 on a card vote. Many delegates felt that for the TUC to adopt a resolution calling for abortion on demand was both offensive to many trade unionists and outside the functions of Congress.

The opposite view is held by Charter members, who are usually active unionists themselves. They believe that the TUC is unlikely to throw its weight behind, for instance, better nursery facilities or greatly improved maternity benefit. Furthermore women in the trade union movement are conscious that the TUC first supported equal pay in 1888 and never pushed it emphatically.

However there were signs within months of the *Equal Pay Act* coming into force at the end of 1975 that some unions and their branches were vigorously supporting members in equal pay claims, even supporting strikes among members to get equal pay. TASS (the white collar section of the engineering union) is particularly active on behalf of women members and USDAW, the retail workers union, also supported members who brought equal pay cases before the industrial tribunals.

One other important indication of the growing confidence of women trade unionists is the number of women nominated by trade unions to serve on industrial tribunals. Ethel Chipchase, women's officer of the TUC pointed out that in this respect, the unions were well in advance of the employers' side which has far fewer women to choose from.

The growth in women's membership of trade unions in recent years reflects both the movement of women out of the house and the growing awareness of their economic power. The impact of female membership is still largely localized, in individual unions, and if women are to achieve full equality at work, they must use the trade union movement. The *Equal Pay Act*, whatever its weaknesses, has already had an impact on women workers and many unions are beginning to realize this. If women learn this lesson – that they can alter the conditions of their working lives – their future influence on trade unionism could be unlimited.

References

ASSOCIATION OF ASSISTANT MISTRESSES IN SECONDARY SCHOOLS (1976) *Promotion of Women Teachers*. London.

ASSOCIATION OF TEACHERS IN TECHNICAL INSTITUTIONS (1973) *The Education, Training and Employment of Women and Girls*. London.

BAETJER, A. (1948) *Women in Industry*. Philadelphia: W. B. Saunders & Co.

BEETON, Mrs (1861) *Book of Household Management*. London: Cape.

BECON (1543) *Boke of Matrimony*.

BELBIN, E. (1964) *Training the Adult Worker*. London: HMSO.

BELBIN, E. and BELBIN, R. Meredith (1972) *Problems in Adult Retraining*. London: Heinemann.

BENTON, S. (1975) *Patterns of Discrimination Against Women in the Film and Television Industries.* ACTT Special Report. London.

BEST, G. (1973) *Mid Victorian Britain.* London: Panther.

BLACKSTONE, T. (1971) *A Fair Start.* Harmondsworth: Allen Lane, the Penguin Press.

BRISTOL, University of (1973) National Study of Child Health and Education in the 1970s. Preliminary (unpublished) results of the regional Survey.

BROOKS, S. (1972) Comment. *Social Work Today,* July.

BROWN, M. (1974) *Sweated Labour.* London: Low Pay Unit.

BROWN, M. and WINYARD, S. (1975) *Low Pay in Hotels and Catering.* London: Low Pay Unit.

BURNETT, J. (ed.) (1974) *Useful Toil.* Harmondsworth: Penguin Books.

CENTRAL OFFICE OF INFORMATION (1975) *Women in Britain.* London: COI.

CENTRAL STATISTICAL OFFICE (1974) *Social Trends.* London: HMSO.

CIVIL SERVICE DEPARTMENT (1971) *The Employment of Women in the Civil Service.* London: HMSO.

CLARK, A. (1919) *The Working Life of Women in the Seventeenth Century.* London: George Routledge & Sons.

CLOTHING AND ALLIED PRODUCTS INDUSTRIAL TRAINING BOARD (1973) *In Lieu of School Leavers.*

CLOTHING ECONOMIC DEVELOPMENT COUNCIL (1972) *What the Girls Think!* London: National Economic Development Council.

COMER, L. (1974) *Wedlocked Women.* Leeds: Feminist Books.

COMMISSION ON INDUSTRIAL RELATIONS (1973) *Homeworkers.* London: HMSO.

COMMITTEE ON HIGHER EDUCATION (1963) *Higher Education* (Robbins Report). London: HMSO.

COMMONS, HOUSE OF (1973) *The Employment of Women.* Report VI of the Expenditure Committee. London: HMSO.

CONRAN, S. (1975) *Superwoman.* London: Sidgwick & Jackson.

COOTE, A. (1976) The Pay's not the Same. *Observer,* June 6.

COOTE, A. and GILL, T. (1974) *Women's Rights:* A Practical Guide. Harmondsworth: Penguin Books.

COUNTER INFORMATION SERVICES (1976) *Women under Attack.* Anti Report no. 15.

DAWES, F. (1973) *Not in Front of the Servants*. London: Wayland Publishers.

DOUGLAS, J. W. B., ROSS, J. M., and SIMPSON, S. R. (1968) *All Our Future*. London: Peter Davies.

DRAKE, B. (1918) *Women in the Engineering Trade*. London: Allen and Unwin and Labour Research Department.

EDUCATION AND SCIENCE, Department of (1973) *Careers Education in Secondary Schools*. London: HMSO.

—— (1975) *Curricular Differences for Boys and Girls*. Education Survey no. 21. London: HMSO.

EMPLOYMENT, DEPARTMENT OF (1969) *Hours of Employment of Women and Young Persons Employment in Factories*. London: HMSO.

—— (1973) *Gazette*. October.

—— (1974, 1975, 1976) *New Earnings Survey*. London: HMSO.

—— (1974) *Women and Work. A Statistical Survey*. Manpower Paper No 9. London: HMSO.

—— (1975) *Women and Work. A Review*. Manpower Paper No. 10. London: HMSO.

—— (1974a) *Women and Work. Sex Differences and Society*. Manpower Paper No. 11. London: HMSO.

—— (1975) *Women and Work. Overseas Practice*. Manpower Paper No. 12. London: HMSO.

—— (1975) *Gazette*. August.

FIGES, E. (1972) *Patriarchal Attitudes*. London: Panther.

FITZHERBERT, Sir Anthony (1555) *Boke of Husbandrie*.

FLETCHER, R. (1966) *The Family and Marriage in Britain*. Harmondsworth: Pelican Books.

FOGARTY, M. (1967) *Women and Top Jobs*. London: PEP.

FONDA, N. (1976) Maternity Leave. *Personnel Management*, January.

FRIEDAN, B. (1965) *The Feminine Mystique*. Harmondsworth: Penguin Books.

GARDINER, J. (1975) Women's Domestic Labour. *New Left Review* (89), Jan–Feb.

GASKELL, P. (1968) *Artisans and Machinery: Moral and Physical Condition of the Manufacturing Population*. London: Frank Cass.

GAVRON, H. (1966) *The Captive Wife*. Harmondsworth: Penguin Books.

GOVERNMENT ACTUARY DEPARTMENT (1971) *Occupational Pensions Scheme.* London: HMSO.

GOVERNMENT, H. M. (1974) *Report on One Parent Families* (Finer Report). London: HMSO.

GREER, G. (1971) *The Female Eunuch.* London: Paladin.

GREGORY, E. (1969) *Child Minding in Paddington.* London: Community Relations Commission.

HAGGER, A. (1973) Recruiting School Mums. *Industrial and Commercial Training.*

HAMILTON, M. (1928) *Mary Macarthur.* London: Leonard Parson.

HEALTH AND SOCIAL SECURITY, DEPARTMENT OF (1974, 1975) *Health and Social Services Statistics for England.* London: HMSO.

HEWITT, P. (ed.) (1974) *Danger – Women at Work.* London: National Council for Civil Liberties.

—— (1975) *Rights for Women.* London: NCCL.

HOME OFFICE (1975) *A Guide to the Sex Discrimination Act.* London: HMSO.

HORTON, T. (1975) Nil Growth and the Nursery Programme. *Primary Education Review* No. 1.

HOTEL AND CATERING INDUSTRY TRAINING BOARD (1974) *Employment Patterns of Graduates in Hotel, Catering and Institutional Management Subjects.*

Household Book of Domestic Economy (c. 1850). London: John Dicks.

HUNT, A. (1968) *A Survey of Women's Employment.* London: Department of Employment.

—— (1975) *Management Attitudes and Practices Towards Women at Work.* London: Office of Population Censuses and Surveys.

INCOMES DATA SERVICES LTD (1973) *Maternity Leave.* Study no. 58. London.

—— (1973) *Part-Time Work.* Study no. 62. London.

—— (1974) *Women's Pay.* Study no. 79. London.

—— (1975) *Women's Pay and Employment.* Study no. 100. London.

—— (1976) *Reports,* nos. 225, 227, 229, 230. London.

INNER LONDON EDUCATION AUTHORITY (1975) *Career Opportunities for Women and Girls.* London: ILEA.

INSTITUTE OF MANPOWER STUDIES (1974) *People and*

Jobs in Distribution. London: Manpower Services Commission.

INSTITUTE OF PERSONNEL MANAGEMENT (1975) *Company Nurseries.* London: IPM.

KELLY, A. (1975) A Discouraging Process. How Girls are Eased Out of Science. Paper presented at the Girls and Science Education Conference, Edinburgh University.

KING, J. S. (1973) Construction and Standardization of the Department of Employment Vocational Assessment Test (DEVAT) Series. Dept. of Employment internal publication.

KINNERSLEY, P. (1974) *Hazards of Work: How to Fight Them.* London: Pluto Press.

KNIGHT, P. (1974) *The Successful Applicant Will be a Man.* London: British Humanist Association.

LAMB, F. and PICKTHORN, H. (1968) *Locked-Up Daughters.* London: Hodder and Stoughton.

MANPOWER RESEARCH UNIT (1968) *Occupational Change 1951–61.* Manpower Studies No. 6. London: Department of Employment.

MEPHAM, G. J. (1969) *Problems of Equal Pay.* London: Institute of Personnel Management.

—— (1974) *Equal Opportunity and Equal Pay.* London: Institute of Personnel Management.

MILLER, R. (1973) *Careers for Girls.* Harmondsworth: Penguin Books.

MITCHELL, J. (1971) *Women's Estate.* Harmondsworth: Pelican Books.

MOOREHEAD, C. (1975) Every Woman's Brief for a Case of Unlawful Discrimination. *The Times* December 3.

NANDY, D. and L. (1975) Towards True Equality for Women. *New Society,* 30 January.

NATIONAL CHILDRENS BUREAU (1973) *Children of Working Mothers.* Highlight No. 2. April. London.

NATIONAL COUNCIL FOR CIVIL LIBERTIES (1975) Women Factory Workers (pamphlet). London.

—— (1975) *Equal Pay and How to Get It.* London.

NATIONAL ECONOMIC DEVELOPMENT OFFICE (1974) *Manpower and Pay in Retail Distribution.* London: NEDC.

NATIONAL AND LOCAL GOVERNMENT OFFICERS ASSOCIATION (1975) *Equal Rights Working Party Report.* London: NALGO.

NATIONAL PRICES AND INCOMES BOARD (1971) *General Problems of Low Pay*. London: HMSO.

NOBLE LOWNDES (1975) *Guide to the Social Security Pensions Act. For Better or Worse*.

NEWSOM, J. (1948) *The Education of Girls*. London: Faber and Faber.

OAKLEY, A. (1974) *The Sociology of Housework*. London: Martin Robertson.

OLIVER, T. (ed.) (1902) *Dangerous Trades. Historical, Social and Legal Aspects of Industrial Occupations Affecting Health*. London: John Murray.

PERSONNEL MANAGEMENT (1970) The Industrial Benefits of the Nursery. March.

PIDGEON, D. (1970) *Expectation and Pupil Performance*. Windsor, Berks: National Foundation for Educational Research.

PINCHBECK, I. (1969) *Women Workers in the Industrial Revolution*. London: Frank Cass.

PRICE, D. G. (1973) The Experimental Introduction of the Department of Employment Vocational Tests (DEVAT) into the Youth Employment Service. Department of Employment internal publication.

ROBINSON, O. and WALLACE, J. (1973) Study of Earnings of Part Time Workers in Retailing. University of Bath School of Management.

ROWBOTHAM, S. (1973) *Hidden from History*. London: Pluto Press.

ROYAL COLLEGE OF NURSING (1972) *Report of Committee on Nursing*. London: HMSO.

SEEAR, N. (1971) *Re-Entry of Women into the Labour Market After an Interruption in Employment*. Paris: OECD.

SOUTHGATE, H. (1887) *Things a Lady Would Like to Know*. London: W. P. Nimmo.

STANDING CONFERENCE OF UNIVERSITY APPOINTMENT SERVICES (1975) Report on 'Equal Opportunities for Women'. Careers Centre, University of East Anglia.

STAFFORD, A. (1961) *A Match to Fire the Thames*. London: Hodder & Stoughton.

TASS (Technical and Supervisory Section of the Amalgamated Union of Engineering Workers) (1975) *Women's Rights and What We Are Doing to Get Them*. London.

TATTERSALL, E. (1975) Women at Work at Rise. *Science for People* 29.

THOMPSON, F. (1973) *Lark Rise to Candleford*. Harmondsworth: Penguin Books.

TIZARD, J., PERRY, J., and MOSS, P. (1976) *All Our Children*. London: Temple Smith.

TRADES UNION CONGRESS (1955) *Women and the Trade Union Movement*. London.

—— (1972) *The Roots of Inequality*. London.

—— (1973, 1974, 1975) Reports of the Women's Conferences. London.

TRADES UNION RESEARCH UNIT (1975) *Equal Pay: A Critical Review of Progress*. Ruskin College, Oxford.

TRAINING SERVICES AGENCY (1975) *Training Opportunities for Women*. London: Manpower Services Commission.

—— (1975) *Vocational Preparation for Young People*. London: Manpower Services Commission.

TURNER, B. (1974) *Equality for Some*. London: Ward Lock.

WALTON, R. (1975) *Women in Social Work*. London: Routledge & Kegan Paul.

WATSON, J. (1970) *The Double Helix*. Harmondsworth: Penguin Books.

WOBER, M. (1971) *English Girls' Boarding Schools*. Harmondsworth: Allen Lane, The Penguin Publishers.

WOMEN'S LIBERATION CAMPAIGN FOR LEGAL AND FINANCIAL INDEPENDENCE (1975) *The Demand for Independence*, November.

WOODHAM-SMITH, C. (1952) *Florence Nightingale*. London: The Reprint Society.

YAGER, J. W. (1973) Congenital Malformations and Environmental Influences: the Occupational Environment of Laboratory Workers. *Journal of Occupational Medicine* (9).

YOUNG, M. and WILLMOTT, P. (1957) *Family and Kinship in East London*. London: Routledge & Kegan Paul.

YUDKIN, S. and HOLME, A. (1963) *Working Mothers and Their Children*. London: Michael Joseph.

Name Index

Armstrong, Ernest, 33

Subject Index